Southport's Secret Suffragist

Southport's Secret Suffragist

The Story of
Anna Alene Clemmons

ELIZABETH STANFORD FULLER, PHD

This book is based on real people and real events in Southport (Smithville) and other parts of North Carolina from the 1850s through the 1950s. Parts of the story have been dramatized. As no record exists of the actual thoughts, opinions, and detailed actions of Miss Anna Clemmons or her family, these have, by necessity, been drawn from the author's imagination.

Front cover image created with DALLE-3

First printing edition 2024 in the United States

Southport Historical Society
P.O. Box 10014
Southport, North Carolina 28461
www.southporthistoricalsociety.org

To Bob

It should not be necessary to struggle forever against popular prejudice, and with us as colored women, this struggle becomes two-fold, first, because we are women and second because we are colored women.

Mary Bennett Talbert
President,
National Association
of Colored Women.
Oberlin class of 1889

TABLE OF CONTENTS

A NOTE FROM THE AUTHOR VI

A PLAY IN ONE ACT 1

READING GROUP DISCUSSION GUIDE..44

FREQUENTLY ASKED QUESTIONS ABOUT THE LIFE OF ANNIE CLEMMONS 47

    HOW DID THE CLEMMONS FAMILY COME TO LIVE IN SOUTHPORT?...................48

    HOW DID ALLEN CLEMMONS SUPPORT HIS FAMILY?......................................51

    WHERE DID THE CLEMMONS FAMILY LIVE? 53

    DID ALLEN CLEMMONS AND OTHER BLACK MEN IN SMITHVILLE VOTE?...........56

    WHAT WAS ANNIE'S LIFE LIKE AS A CHILD IN SOUTHPORT? 65

    WHAT WAS ANNIE'S CAREER LIKE? 71

    WHAT WAS ANNIE LIKE AS A MOTHER? 74

    WHAT WAS THE REACTION IN SOUTHPORT TOWARD WOMEN VOTING?............77

    WHAT WAS ANNIE CLEMMONS' REACTION TO THE 19TH AMENDMENT? 81

    WAS ANNIE RIGHT TO BE CONCERNED ABOUT THE THREAT OF A LAWLESS MOB? 86

    WHAT WAS ANNIE'S LIFE LIKE IN HER LATER YEARS? 88

    WHERE IS ANNIE'S FINAL RESTING PLACE?..90

    WHAT HAPPENED TO ANNIE'S DAUGHTER?...91

    WHAT HAPPENED TO THE REST OF ANNIE CLEMMONS' FAMILY? 95

FREQUENTLY ASKED QUESTIONS ABOUT NC BLACK VOTING RIGHTS . 98

    HOW DID NC BLACK MEN OBTAIN THE RIGHT TO VOTE?................................99

    HOW DID THE NC KU KLUX KLAN TRY TO STOP BLACK VOTERS? 105

    HOW DID NC'S GOVERNMENT TRY TO STOP BLACK MEN FROM VOTING? 113

    WHAT HAPPENED TO NC BLACK VOTERS WHEN RECONSTRUCTION ENDED? 118

    WHAT WAS THE WILMINGTON MASSACRE OF 1898? 123

    HOW DID NC'S LITERACY TEST KEEP BLACK CITIZENS FROM VOTING?.............129

CONCLUSION...134

    DID ANNIE'S LETTERS HELP GUARANTEE VOTING RIGHTS FOR BLACK CITIZENS? 135

ACKNOWLEDGEMENTS...139

TIMELINE OF THIS BOOK..143

BIBLIOGRAPHY AND ENDNOTES 146

List of Photos and Illustrations

FIGURE 1 THE CREW OF THE U.S. ENGINEERS DREDGE CAPE FEAR CIRCA 1914. 52

FIGURE 2 MAP OF THE ORIGINAL 100 LOTS IN SMITHVILLE. 55

FIGURE 3 FRANK GORDON, BRUNSWICK COUNTY EDUCATOR. 61

FIGURE 4 ALLEN CLEMMONS... 65

FIGURE 5 BRUNSWICK COUNTY TRAINING SCHOOL#1 87

FIGURE 6 ANNIE CLEMMONS' GRAVE 91

FIGURE 7 ANNIE CLEMMONS' COMMEMORATIVE BRICK. 91

FIGURE 8 LOUISE CLEMMONS DOOLEY AND WALTER A. DOOLEY. 94

FIGURE 9 CONGRESSIONAL DISTRICT MAPS BASED ON THE 1870 U.S. CENSUS. 114

FIGURE 10 FOUR CONGRESSMEN FROM NC DISTRICT TWO. 115

FIGURE 11 ANNIE CLEMMONS OBITUARY.. 115

A Note from the Author

This book is written in two parts. The first part is a dramatization of Annie Clemmon's life story. It is written as though Annie were sitting in her home toward the end of her life, talking to visitors.

As I researched Annie's life, I was struck by how much she wanted her voice to be heard. But the extenuating circumstances under which she lived forced her to keep her story secret. The more I reflected on Annie's situation, the more I wished that she had been able to tell her story, hence the idea for the play.

To create the play, I had to fill in the gaps in the historical record with my best guesses as to what she and her parents thought, felt, and did. I hope that I was able to do them justice.

The second part of the book contains the historical information upon which the play is based. Each chapter answers a question that came up during the time I was researching and discussing Annie's life story. These chapters can be read in any sequence, depending on the reader's areas of interest.

Of special note is some of the language in the book. There are words used in the book which are no longer considered appropriate or kind. However, this is a history book, and where the historical records, including Annie's letters, use those terms, I have kept them as written.

Even more than words, there are events in this book that are offensive. I hear concerns these days that history shouldn't be taught if it makes the learner uncomfortable. But it's my view that history, especially the history of offensive acts, ought to make us uncomfortable. It means that as a society, we have grown in our morality. The more important concern is what do we do with that discomfort?

So, I hope that readers of this book are offended, and uncomfortable, and morally outraged. And that reading this book will promote conversations about justice, fairness, and the importance of voting and other civil rights. Perhaps it will even prompt some letter writing.

Most of all, I am grateful that through my research I have gotten to know Annie Clemmons a little better. I hope that you enjoy getting to know her, too.

Liz Fuller
December 2023

Elizabeth Stanford Fuller, PhD

Anna Clemmons:

Southport's Secret Suffragist

A Play in One Act

Anna Clemmons:

Southport's Secret Suffragist

A Play in One Act

by

Elizabeth Stanford Fuller

Character

Anna Clemmons: A 65-year-old Southern Black woman. It's apparent that she was strong in her youth but has become more frail in recent years as her health has faded. Despite her infirmity, she retains a quiet dignity. She is dressed in bib overalls and a man's flannel shirt.

Scene

Anna Clemmons' home in Southport, NC

Time

1956

Act 1

SETTING: A summer evening in Southport, North Carolina: A small fishing village at the mouth of the Cape Fear River. The living room of a small, wood-frame home. The walls are unpainted and bare except for the framed portrait of an older Black man (Anna's father). A rocking chair sits in the center of the room. A laundry basket sits next to the chair with a few items of clothing (a nurse's apron, a shawl, and a lady's hat). A small writing desk and chair sit to one side. The desk holds a pen, stationery, and an old newspaper.

AT RISE: ANNA enters from stage right. She moves slowly and a little painfully as though her lower back hurts. As she comes into the room, she pauses to touch some of the items on her desk and to straighten the picture on the wall, taking a moment to gaze lovingly at the picture of her father. Gingerly, she eases herself into the rocking chair and reaches into the basket beside her to pick up some knitting. Only after she is settled does she look up and greet her company.

ANNA

Good evenin'. My name's Anna Alene Clemmons. Most folks call me Miss Annie. Though I can't say everybody called me that.

> (Chuckles to
> herself as she
> remembers.)

See, some years ago, my nephew George Raphael and his wife Mariah lived with me for a little while, along with their little boy, Stevie. Now, that boy, he never did know what to make of me.

Stevie, he used to call me "Mr. Annie" See, he thought I was a man, 'cause I always dressed like this, wearing pants. I guess he thought a woman couldn't wear pants.

I didn't mind.

> (Talking almost to
> herself.)

It wasn't the first time in my life someone tried to tell me what a woman could or couldn't do.

> (Remembers her
> guests and speaks to
> them again.)

This here is my house. I don't suppose it looks like much to you. But it's mine. My papa left me this house when he died. He left the property to me and my youngest brother, Baby −Mama named him John, but we always called him

5

Baby – Papa gave Baby one half of the property – and he left me the other half.

We live here in Southport – side by side on East Brown Street. I never did get around to paintin' the walls. One of my brother George's grandbabies, Priscilla, when she was a little thing, she used to think my house was haunted. She said it looked spooky (chuckles) – what with my bare unpainted walls. But I just never had the time nor the money to get around to paintin'. I was always busy lookin' after this one or the other one. I guess you could say I had different priorities than most folk.

But I don't get out so much anymore. I'm gettin' old. Slowin' down. My kidneys have been botherin' me some. Oh, I know my time is runnin' out. I'm a nurse and I know about these things. My niece Inez, maybe y'all know her? Well, she tends to me sometimes. She's so good to me.

See, I don't have long.

(Notices the
audience's reaction.)

Oh, it's fine. Don't y'all worry. I've lived a long life – I'm 65 years old. And it's been good. It's been good. I've done a lot in my life.

Course there are some things I'd still like to do... Guess I won't get to do them now.

(Rocks a bit in her
chair as she reflects
while she works up
the courage to share
more with her
visitors.)

But before I leave this world, I want to tell my secret. I have been carryin' around a secret for most of my life. At first, I was scared to tell it. And then I thought maybe it wasn't that important. Maybe it didn't matter to nobody but me. But lately, as I sit here, I keep thinkin' about how things used to be, and then I think about how things still are. And it makes me want to tell my secret to somebody. That's why I'm pleased you're here this evenin' – when I'm in a secret-telling mood.

See, all my life, people have been puttin' rules on me – tellin' me what I can do and what I cannot do. Where I can and cannot live, where I can and cannot shop, where I can and cannot go to school, how I can and cannot earn a livin'.

All sorts of rules. I don't understand it. Do you?

But I'll tell you the one that bothers me the most. The one that just rubs me raw. That's the one that says I can't vote.

I can't vote.

It is 1956. And still – I can't vote.

Not too long ago, I was talkin' to a neighbor of mine. He told me that when he got back from servin' in the army in WWII, why he went over to the courthouse to register to vote. He reckoned that after fightin' for this country in the war, he wouldn't have no trouble registerin' to vote.

But the way he told me, when he went to the registrator's office, that registrator told him first he was gonna have to answer a few questions to see if he was eligible. He had to prove that he was literate.

So, the registrator said to him – how many bricks are there in this here courthouse buildin'? And, my neighbor, he said, well, if you tell me the dimensions, I could calculate it. (slaps her thigh and laughs)

Ooh! They didn't like that!

(As her laughter
ends, her smile slowly
fades and she gets
serious.)

So, then that registrator said, how about you tell me how many bubbles are in a bar of soap?

My neighbor, he didn't get registered that day… and if they won't let a WWII army veteran register to vote, you know they ain't gonna let me.

Now, some folks say times are changin'. That the laws and the rules are changin'. That before too long, I will be able to vote, right here in Southport. But I'm runnin' out of time. I can't wait much longer. My kidneys, you know.

(To herself.) Same as Mama.

Besides, I've heard all that kind of talk before. I can remember way back when they first told me the laws were goin' to change. That was thirty-six years ago. Thirty-six years! And I'm still waitin'.

See, one thing I've learned in life is that the only times the laws change fast is when they want to make it harder for folks to do somethin'. When they want to make it easier – well, then it takes a long time.

A long time.

Now I'm old enough to remember when things were different. Most people don't remember now. Or maybe they never knew. But when I was a little girl, things were different. Back then, all the colored men in Brunswick County could vote. Can you believe that?

I remember Papa and Mama. They used to have so much hope. So much hope. For my brothers and my sister and me.

See, I was born in 1890. I was number six. My mama had thirteen babies in all, but only nine of us survived. Seven boys and two girls. And we were all born free.

It was different for Mama and Papa. They were born a long time ago – before the War Between the States. Papa lived on a big farm over in Lockwood's Folly and Mama lived right here in Southport, with the minister's family.

Papa was a Clemmons, and Mama was an Evans. Mama was just a little bitty thing when the war ended. Maybe seven. Papa was ten or twelve. He said he'll never forget when the soldiers came and told them they were free.

'Course, Mama, and Papa didn't know for sure exactly how old they were because, you know, no one ever told them exactly when they were born. So, after the war, after he was free, since Papa didn't know when his birthday was – he just picked his own birthday.

Y'all know what day he picked? The 4th of July. That's right. Same day as the birthday of the United States of America. That's how proud Papa was to be a citizen.

So, after they grew up, and seein' as they were free, Mama and Papa got married. They had a piece of paper that proved they were husband and wife. They sure were proud of that piece of paper.

See – there wasn't anythin' like that when they were growin' up. Slaves could say they were married – in their hearts, you know – but there weren't any legal papers to prove it.

So, after they were married, Papa started workin' for the United States government. Every mornin' he'd get up before the sun. He and the other men in the neighborhood would walk together, down to the river to work. I'd lie in bed and hear them talkin' and jokin' with each other. Teasin' this one for lookin' so sleepy, and that one for bein' so skinny that his pants wouldn't stay up.

In the mornin's, they tried to keep quiet because they knew the babies were still in bed. But in the evenin's, when their work was done, they didn't worry about makin' noise. I could hear them walkin' home from blocks away. They'd be singin' and laughin' and pokin' fun. I'd stop whatever chore I was doin' and run in my bare feet down the path to catch up with Papa. When he saw me, he'd bend down and scoop me up in his arms and swing me up in the air.

No matter how tired he was from workin', he'd always carry me back home in his arms.

Papa was so proud of his job. He worked on the U.S. government dredge boat. It was named the Cape Fear. Just like the river. All day long, it would go up and down the river, scoopin' up the sand and makin' it easier for the boats to get up and down the river to Wilmington.

> (Pauses. Her eyes
> light up. Her voice
> becomes reverent.)

Wilmington!!

Have y'all ever been to Wilmington?

When I was a little bitty girl, Papa used to tell me all sorts of stories about Wilmington. You know, back then, it was the biggest city in all of North Carolina. And it had everythin' – telephones and electric lights and street cars.

Imagine!

But the best thing about Wilmington was the opportunity. That's what Papa told me.

He said in Wilmington, there were colored men who worked all kinds of jobs – there were teachers and lawyers, and businessmen! They had real school buildin's for colored children – not just rooms in churches. Did you know there were more colored folk livin' in Wilmington than white folk? And some of them worked jobs right alongside the white folk – like in the post office or as policemen or for the customs office.

Papa said Wilmington was just burstin' with opportunity. 'Course, we had some of that opportunity here in Southport too. Papa didn't just own our house on Brown Street. He also owned a farm just outside of town. So did the Jacksons and the Griffins and some others. There was a whole community. Some farmed full-time, and others, like Papa, worked on the river or at the sawmill as their main job and then did farmin' on the side. Women and children worked on the farm too. Everybody did what they could.

Growin' your own food was the best way to feed your family. And most of the women also took in laundry or cleaned and cooked for the white folks that lived in town. It wasn't easy, but they were happy. They could be together in their own house. And Mama knew that nobody could come along and sell her husband or her babies away from her.

But even though that was good, they wanted more for their children. Whenever Mama and Papa talked about the possibility of things to come, they would say, *just look what's happenin' in Wilmington!*

Papa was proud of his job and his home and his family. But he was especially proud of bein' able to vote. On election day he would put on his church clothes and walk into town to make his vote. He said that's what was special about bein' an American, about bein' free. He said votin' is how you make your voice heard.

I remember real clearly the election of 1898. I was eight years old. Papa told Mama he was goin' downtown to make his vote.

Now, Mama, she was kind of anxious. See, there had been rumors that there might be some trouble. But Papa told her she shouldn't listen to no gossip. No one was gonna stop him from votin'.

I asked if I could go with him. I wanted to see him vote. But he told me no. It was no place for children. So, I just stood outside and watched him as he walked down the path. His back – tall and straight. I watched all the way until he disappeared out of sight.

(Pauses to rock a
bit and remember.)

That night, when Papa came home, I could tell he was upset. Mama could too. She told me to go outside and dig up some sweet potatoes for supper. But you know, I just went as far as the doorway, and then I hid myself so's I could listen.

I knew it was wrong to listen – but I couldn't help myself. I wanted to know what made Papa's face look that way.

That's how I heard what Papa told Mama. He told her that the white men in Southport had thrown the colored men's votes away. He said that all the colored men's votes were printed on yellow paper. That's what they had told them to use. But at the end of the day, when they went to count the votes, they said, "What's this? Yellow votes? These ain't right. We can't count 'em."

And they just threw them away.

I peeked around the doorway. Papa was sittin' in a chair. He didn't see me because he was leanin' forward with his elbows on his knees and holdin' his head in his hands. He said, "It ain't right. It just ain't right."

Mama was standin' beside him. Her eyes were shut tight, and she was slowly shakin' her head back and forth like she just didn't want to picture what he was describin'. She just patted him on his shoulder. She said, "Don't mind that now. There'll be other elections. Next time you'll use the right paper. It'll all work out fine."

> (Annie rocks some
> more. A little harder
> this time.)

The next day, it was more quiet around here than usual. Folks were talkin' in hushed voices. They tried not to let me hear but I was real good at stayin' out of sight. They talked about the election and how the white men just threw away the votes.

There wasn't any singin' or laughin' that day.

> (Rocks more. Hums
> a little under her
> breath. Building up
> her courage to
> continue.)

We thought that day was bad. But we had no idea of what was comin' next.

See, two days after the election, Captain Harper's steamboat brought news down from Wilmington. I was sittin' on the front porch shellin' peas when Papa came home from work. He surprised me. I hadn't even heard him comin' up the path. He just marched right up to the house and walked past me without so much as a hello. He went in to talk to Mama.

They were both so upset that they plum forgot that I was sittin' there on the porch. They didn't even try to whisper. So, I just kept quiet and stayed real still. And that way, I heard everythin' that Papa said.

It seems that somethin' awful had happened in Wilmington. The white men had gotten real mad at the colored folk. It had somethin' to do with the election. Or maybe somethin' to do with all the opportunity. I didn't know for sure. But anyhow, the white men burned down the colored newspaper office. Then they must of still been mad because they marched over to the colored part of town, and they commenced to shootin'.

Papa said nobody knows how many men they killed. Maybe dozens. They just left their bodies lyin' in the streets. They even threw some of the bodies into the Cape Fear River. The women and children were so scared they ran off into the swamps to hide. Even though it was cold and they were hungry, they were too afraid to go back to their homes.

Papa said it was a massacre.

Mama just cried and cried. She begged Papa not to leave the house – not to go to work. She didn't want my brothers to go to work neither. She was afraid they would get shot. She was scared she'd lose the children she had left.

She said, *Just look what's happenin' in Wilmington!*

But Papa said he had a job with the United States government. And he was goin' to go to work. No one was goin' to stop him. And the next mornin', he and the other men got up early and walked down the road to town. I was still in bed, but I was awake. I heard their footsteps as they walked down the street. There wasn't any teasin'. There wasn't any laughin'. They were just shadows in the moonlight headin' for the river.

> (She stops rocking.
> Lost in the
> memory. Slowly
> comes back to the
> present day.)

Papa didn't get shot. There wasn't any fightin' in Southport. Little by little, life got better. Sometimes I still saw Mama wipe a tear from her eye when she thought no one was lookin'. But she didn't cry in front of Papa no more. And after a while, Papa started to teasin' and laughin' again. But I could tell he didn't think things were as funny as they once were.

Seems like, after the trouble in Wilmington, things just kept gettin' worse and worse. Word went around that the laws were changin'. They made new rules about votin'.

Southport's Secret Suffragist

They said colored men would only be able to vote if they could read and write. When Papa heard that, it was like a light went right out of his eyes. You see, he had never learned to read or write. All his life, he'd been too busy workin' and providin' for his family.

Before the war had set us free, back durin' slavery times, it was against the law for colored folk in North Carolina to so much as look at a book. Then after he was free, Papa was too busy workin' to go to school. But Mama, she learned a little. And Mama and Papa made sure us children learned.

About that time, my oldest brother, Allen, was old enough to vote. He had been to school. He could read and write real good. He went down to the courthouse to register. But they told him no. They said his readin' and writin' weren't good enough. He wasn't allowed to vote.

That made me mad. Up until then, I had been too little to go to school. I was still stayin' home with Mama and helpin' her take care of my three baby brothers. But right then, I made up my mind. I would learn to read and write. I would learn real good. I wouldn't let nobody tell me I couldn't do it good enough.

So, I told Mama it was time for me to go to school. And she must have seen somethin' stubborn in my eyes – because just like that – she let me go.

After that, it seemed like laws changed real fast. With none of the colored folk votin', we didn't have a say in what the laws were or who was in charge. We just had to learn the rules and remember what they were so we wouldn't get in trouble. Seems like as soon as I thought I had learned all the rules – they added some more.

> (Reciting to herself
> in a singsong, rocking
> in time.)

That store's for White folks only. Never go to the front door – only use the back door. Step aside, move off the sidewalk, lower your eyes, Keep your head down. Yes ma'am. No ma'am. Don't make trouble.

> (Stops rocking.)

Look what happened in Wilmington!

> (As she speaks, she
> reaches for the
> nurse's apron in the
> basket then slowly
> stands up from the
> chair and gets her
> balance.)

After a while, I grew up, and I finished goin' to school. In fact, I became a teacher myself. And I liked it fine. I was glad to help support my family. But after a couple of years, I started doin' some nursin', and I liked that even better.

(Ties the nurse's
apron on over her
overalls. She appears
taller and stronger
now with the apron on
and as she reflects on
her nursing
experience.)

See, back then, we didn't have no hospital. Not in all of
Brunswick County. There was just Dr. Watson at the
pharmacy and Dr. Dosher at the quarantine station. A
couple other doctors came and went over the years, but
they were the two main ones.

Do y'all know Dr. Dosher? I guess he was just about the
finest surgeon in the South. And sometimes, he let me
help him with his patients. He taught me a lot about carin'
for sick folk.

'Course, I already knew a lot that I had learned from
Mama like how to gather wormwood and brew a tea that'd
soothe your stomach or break a fever.

Suppose you had a stubborn splinter deep in your finger,
why I knew to tie a piece of fatback around it before you
went to bed. In the mornin', that splinter would of been
pulled right out of your finger and settled in that old
fatback.

And, if you got a cut, I could stop the bleedin' by usin' a
few spiderwebs as a bandage. Oh, I knew a lot already.

And Dr. Dosher he taught me even more from what he learned at that school he went to up north in Maryland.

I surely did like nursin' even better than teachin'.

Then, when I was about twenty-three, the most important event of my life happened.

I had a baby. (Big smile.)

I didn't have a husband. I never did get married. But that was just fine with me. I figured, if I didn't have a husband, then I wouldn't have to worry about losin' him. But I had my baby. A little girl. I named her Maggie Louise. But we all called her Little Baby.

She was the prettiest little thing you ever saw. She had fair skin and light brown eyes. She looked like a little baby doll, and I loved takin' care of her.

> (Pause. Lost in
> memory. Then returns
> to the present.)

Anyways, I'd always been real careful with money, and about a year after Little Baby was born, Dr. Swasey from up North, he sold me a piece of land over on Lord Street where I built a house. It was just the right size for Little Baby and me. We were real happy there.

> (Starts pacing as
> she talks.)

I guess that was sometime around 1914, 'cause right about then, folks started talkin' about fightin' goin' on in Europe, way over across the ocean. At first, I didn't pay no never mind. I was too busy with my nursin' and my housekeepin' and bein' a mama. I didn't want to hear about no war in another country.

But then, when Little Baby was about four years old, they started to draftin' American men to go fight in that war. Dr. Dosher, he left town. He went on a ship all the way across the ocean, to a country by the name of France – so he could save soldiers' lives over there.

And me? I joined the Red Cross. See, we had two Red Crosses in Southport. One was for us coloreds, and the other was for the white ladies. Mostly we'd just get together and roll bandages to send to the army.

We also helped with the enlistment because the government said that all the men in the country had to register for the draft. There was a special day for it. We set ourselves up in front of the courthouse. The white ladies from the Woman's Club, they helped to register the white men. And our Red Cross nurses, we helped register the colored men. They came from all over Brunswick County.

Now remember, I had seven brothers.

(Counts on her
fingers.)

Allen, Charlie, Ezra, Joseph, George, Jeremy (his real name was James Franklin, but we all called him Jeremy), and, of course, Baby.

All seven of my brothers filled out their registration cards, and they signed their names. Their full names. Not one of them gave their mark.

And I remember thinkin' to myself how they wouldn't let my brothers register to vote – but they sure were willin' to let them register to fight.

Well, most of my brothers were too old, and they were married, and they had children – so they didn't get drafted to go to war. And Baby, well he was too young. But Jeremy, he was twenty-one, and he didn't have a wife. He was drafted and went to serve in the 349th Labor Battalion, Company D.

Oh, he looked so handsome in his uniform. We were all proud of him for servin' our country. 'Course Mama cried somethin' fierce when he left. She was afraid he would get killed in the fightin', and she would never see him again.

But before Jeremy could go across the ocean to France, the army sent him to Camp Greene in Charlotte. They wanted to teach him how to be a soldier. I remember he left in August of 1918. And how just a few weeks after that, all the soldiers started gettin' sick with somethin' they were callin' the Spanish Flu.

Lots and lots of the soldiers at Camp Greene got sick. Even more of the colored soldiers took sick than the whites. The army said that was because the colored soldiers were just naturally weaker and more sickly than the white soldiers. But I think it's because they had to sleep outside in the tents instead of in the barracks. And also because they didn't have as many doctors and nurses in the colored part of the hospital as in the white part.

Mama was worried that Jeremy was goin' to get hisself killed fightin' in the war. But I worried he wasn't even goin' to make it to France. That Spanish flu would get him right here in North Carolina.

Now about that same time, I had my hands full right here in Southport. The Spanish flu had come here too. They said it was everywhere in the whole world at the same time. People were sick everywhere, all at once. It was somethin' they called an epidemic.

Why, over on Oak Island, at the army base at Fort Caswell, hundreds of the soldiers were gettin' sick, just like at Fort Greene. The army wouldn't let anyone come or go from the Fort. They even stopped Captain Harper's steamship from deliverin' the mail from Wilmington.

Dr. Watson, he put a notice in the newspaper and asked everyone to stop doin' business between Southport and Wilmington. He said with all that travelin' around, people were only goin' to bring more sickness down here to Southport. He said that business could just wait. People's lives were more important.

But you know, people didn't listen. They never do. So, the sickness came down here too. They closed the schools and the churches – and the stores were only open a few hours a day. Seems like the only ones who were workin' were us nurses. Since the schoolteachers didn't have any children to teach, they started helpin' out with the nursin' too.

See, the doctors didn't know what to do. There weren't any medicines that could fix this sickness. Dr. Watson said we could try usin' some Vicks VapoRub to help the sick folk breathe. But that VapoRub was hard to come by. People were buyin' it as fast as it came in the stores.

There was just a whole lot of sickness right here in Southport.

Even Dr. Watson came down with the flu. And everybody at the post office. I was so busy, first helpin' at one house and then at the next. Seems like there was sickness in every single house. There was nothin' I could do for those sick folk but to try and ease their sufferin'. I helped keep 'em clean and fed, and I tried my best to ease their pain.

Sometimes I'd cut an onion in half and set it out in the sick room. That onion would draw the sickness away.

Well, here in Southport, we were lucky. Maybe it was my nursin'. Maybe it was our good healthy breezes. I don't know. But that first time the flu came through, back in the

Fall of 1918, I know that none of the white folk in town passed away.

Can't say the same for the colored folk. Miss Rhoda Stratman, she passed. Left six little children behind. Such a shame. Her husband, Joe, he never did remarry.

Out at the fort, it was different. Almost five hundred soldiers took sick. Seven of them died. Most of those soldiers were far away from home. The army sent their bodies back to their families, on the train.

But one of the men who died was Miss Katie Piver's husband, name of Sgt. Robert Farmer. She buried him here in Southport, in the white folks' buryin' ground. A few months later, when the flu came back around, why Miss Katie's little baby boy died too. She buried him right next to his papa.

Those were some sad days. Some very sad days. But as bad as it was here, it was so much worse over in Wilmington and up at Fort Greene where my brother Jeremy was.

Now my memory ain't what it used to be, but it seems to me like the war and that first wave of the flu went away about the same time. 'Cause a few weeks later, right before Christmas, the army sent my brother Jeremy back home.

When he climbed down off of that train, Mama cried even harder than she had when he left. And Papa, well, he didn't say much – but we could tell he was proud.

What with the war endin' and the flu passin', we thought at last things would get better. But don't you know, as soon as winter started, that Spanish flu came back worse than ever. That time it took both of Dr. Watson's grown sons. I don't think he was ever the same after that.

It surely was a hard time to be a doctor, and it was an even harder time to be a nurse. But Lord knows I did my best. After it was all over, I got a certificate from the North Carolina government for my heroics. They sent me a paper with my name written right on it. It said it was for my heroic service to my community.

Ain't that somethin'?

When I was growin' up, Mama always told me that bad things come in threes. First, there was the war, then there was the epidemic, and then, well, Mama took sick. No, it wasn't the flu. It was her kidneys. They were just wore out.

So, me and Little Baby gave up our little home on Lord Street and moved back in here with Mama and Papa. And I looked after her – right up until the end. After all, I was a nurse, and I was glad to do for her after all the years she'd done for me.

Southport's Secret Suffragist

Mama passed in 1919, the year after that first World War. She was sixty-one years old. She had had thirteen babies, and she buried four of them. All durin' her life, she worried, and she fussed, and she cried over us children. But despite everythin' we went through – she just never gave up hope. She always believed that her children would have lives that were better than hers.

Not long after Mama passed, rumors started up that laws were changin' again. But for once, the news was good. Captain Harper's ship that brought the mail down from Wilmington, well, it brought the newspapers too. And don't you know that I read every bit of those papers.

(Picks up the old
newspaper on the
desk and points to the
article.)

There were stories about women who were marchin' in Washington DC. They were called Suffragists. And they were led by a lady by the name of Miss Alice Paul.

Seems Miss Alice and her Suffragists were protestin' – right in front of the White House, where the President lived. They wanted to be able to vote.

Oh, you can bet the menfolk didn't like that at all. Miss Alice even got herself thrown in jail. And some of her Suffragists got arrested and were beat up by the police! And they were white ladies! I never would of believed it if I hadn't read it myself.

But then, after the war was over, President Woodrow Wilson changed his mind about women votin'. He started to agree with Miss Alice and her Suffragists. He said the police were wrong to throw them in jail and to mistreat them. He said that American women were heroes. He said that bein' in the Red Cross and takin' care of things at home helped the menfolk be able to go off and win the war. He said because of all of what they had done, American women deserved the right to vote!

Well now.

And the newspaper said they weren't just talkin' about white women. They were talkin' about colored women too.

Mercy.

That got me started to thinkin'. Maybe things really were goin' to change for the better. Maybe I was goin' to get to vote!

After that, things started to happen pretty fast. In just a year or so, I think maybe 1920, the government passed what they called the 19th Amendment. It said that women were allowed to vote.

Well, when that happened, you can believe there was some celebratin' by the white ladies of Southport. The Woman's Club held meetin's at the Army Navy Club, and ole Mayor Ruark went around congratulatin' all the ladies on what he called their civic duty. It was all very excitin'.

'Course, no one paid no attention to me. No one congratulated me on my right to vote. No one invited me to meetin's to teach me about my civic duty. It was like they never gave me or any of the colored women in Southport any thought.

But I surely did. I gave it a lot of thought.

And here's what I reckoned – The law said women had the right to vote. The President said that the women in the Red Cross and the women who worked at home so's the men could go to war, were heroes. He said they deserved to vote.

I thought – Wasn't I a member of the Red Cross? Hadn't I worked while the men went to war? Didn't I have a certificate thankin' me for my heroics durin' the Spanish Flu? I thought – I am a woman. I am a hero. I can read. I can write. I reckon that means I can vote!

> (As she speaks, she picks up a shawl that had been lyin' on the rocker and puts it around her shoulders. She puts a hat on her head, gloves on her hands, and picks up a purse.)

Before I could change my mind, I put on my best clothes – believe it or not, I used to wear dresses all the time, instead of these here overalls – and I could clean up good when I wanted to. Well, sir, I marched myself over to the courthouse.

I walked right up to that registrator and told him I wanted to register to vote. He looked all grumpy and irritated like I was botherin' him, but I pretended not to notice. Then he handed me a piece of paper and told me to read it – so I did. Then he told me to write down some words he said – so I did.

But then. He said···

> (Her voice catches
> as she relives the
> shame and
> disappointment.)

he said ··· I didn't read and write well enough to suit him.

Just like when my brothers tried to register – that man sent me away.

I slunk back out of that courthouse, my head hangin' low. I felt so ashamed. So small.

But then, I come to find out – there weren't no colored man or woman in all of Brunswick County that could read or write well enough to suit that old registrator.

31

When I found that out, I went from feelin' ashamed to feelin' mad.

Then I thought about my daughter, Little Baby, waitin' for me at home. She was seven years old. Just about the same age I was the last time Papa voted. I remember how proud I was of him when he left our house that mornin' to go vote. And I remember how humiliated he was when they threw his vote in the trash.

And right then, I knew I couldn't give up. I had to keep on tryin' to vote. I had to set an example for Little Baby.

That's when I remembered Miss Alice Paul and her Suffragists in Washington DC. They were strong women. They knew how to get things done. They weren't afraid of nobody. Not jail, not the police, not even the President of the United States. They would know what I should do. They would help me.

And so I marched back home, and I sat down to write them a letter. I had seen in the newspaper that they called themselves the National Woman's Party. So that's who I wrote.

> (Sits down at the
> desk. Reads the letter
> out loud as she's
> writing.)

The National Woman's Party- Washington D.C.

To The Sect. of above Party,

I am an american colored woman property owner in Brunswick County State of North Carolina and am seeking way to vote by mail if there is a way, because a colored person in my county is unable to vote, because they are colored. Please send me information how to send votes or register to general Headquarters by mail before it is too late to register.

am oblige.
(Miss) Anna A. Clemons
Bx 294   Southport N.C.

After I mailed my letter, I was so excited. I just knew Miss Alice and her ladies were goin' to fix everythin' for me. It was goin' to happen. I was goin' to get registered, and then I was goin' to get to vote. I could hardly wait to see Papa's face when I told him.

Every day for nearly two weeks, I went to the post office to check my mail. I tried not to be impatient. The day I got the letter, I raced all the way back home to read it. I couldn't wait to learn what I needed to do to register to vote.

(Pulls a letter out
of the drawer and
reads it out loud. At
first, her voice is
excited and loud but

then it begins to falter
and grow slower and
more anguished as
she understands the
meaning of the
letter.)

My dear Miss Clemons:

Your letter of October 10 inquiring about
registration and voting by mail in North
Carolina has just come in my hands.

Registration must be made in person in North
Carolina and in the precinct in which you
live. It is possible to vote by mail on
applying for a ballot to the county board.
Registrations close on October 23. As you
undoubtedly understand, no one may register or
vote outside of his own precinct.

We have been making inquiries and learn that
colored women are being registered in North
Carolina. Have you tried personally? If not,
will you try to and let us know the result.
Should the registration board refuse to
register you, we shall be glad to look into
the matter and see what can be done about it.
Please be sure to let us know the result of
your attempt to register.

Very sincerely yours,
[Emma Wold]
Headquarters Secretary

What? No! They don't understand. It don't matter that
some other counties in North Carolina are lettin' colored
women register to vote. I live here in Brunswick County.
And in Brunswick County, they ain't lettin' us register.

(Talking to herself,
pacing, wringing her
hands.)

Oh, I need to make them understand. And what do they mean, they're goin' to look into the matter? Are they goin' to tell someone that I wrote them a letter? That won't do. That won't do at all.

So I sat myself down, and I wrote them another letter. This time, I did my best to explain the situation and to tell them about who I am.

(Sits down at the
desk. Reads the letter
as she's writing.)

Miss Emma Wold: Washington, D.C

My Dear Miss Wold:

In reply to your letter, which was duly received yesterday, will take the greatest of pleasure to write you my result, in attempting or trying to register. I went before the registrator Oct 15th and was refused to be registered, as this board requires all colored to be able to read and write to "suit" the registrator, and all persons of colored origin in this whole county have been unable to suit the registrator; North Carolina laws require one to be able to read and write, to register, still we have in our county ones to fill requirements then they are refused.

I hope, and ask if you should have this matter investigated, then please do not let my name be brought into this matter because there is so much prejudice existing until I am most assured I will be a victim of lawless Mob.

To show you I am no agitator, or race leader, I will try to explain just my position. I am a nurse, have nursed in most every home in this town for past 9 years, acting at times as assistant to one of the South's best Surgeons Dr. J Arthur Dosher of this county. I donated to the Red Cross, Volunteered during the epidemic of "1918," "flu," and hold a certificate for heroic services rendered over my State.

I own property, and pay my tax. I am a Christian. I belong to the Methodist Church. I attend to my own business, don't interfere with no race of people, and try to live here as I expect to live when I pass in the great beyond, that is in peace. I have seven (7) brothers, law-abiding, supposed to be citizens, denied the same as myself.

Hoping and resting assured you will not use my name in this matter that I will close.

From
Anna A. Clemons
Bx 294   Southport N.C.

I mailed my second letter but this time I was more fearful than excited. What if Miss Alice decided to investigate, like she said? What if she used my name? What if someone thought I was stirrin' up trouble? Would I be safe? Would Little Baby? Should I be scared? Should I get a gun?

A week or so later, I got a response. This time when I found the letter in my post office box, I slipped it into my pocket. I didn't want anyone to see I had got a letter from Washington D.C. I tried to act like I wasn't in any hurry, but as soon as I got home – I opened it.

>(Pulls another
>letter out of the desk
>and reads.)

My dear Mrs. Clemons:

Your letter of October **24** has just arrived and I hasten to assure you that if we should undertake any investigation of the matter in which it deals, your name will not be used at all.

>(Closes her eyes,
>puts her hand to her
>chest, and gives a
>silent prayer of
>relief.)

We appreciate your sending us the information about registration in your part of North Carolina.

I have called Miss Alice Paul's attention to your letter of October **24** describing the registration conditions for colored women in your neighborhood.

We have been giving the situation in the south a good deal of thought. But at present we see only one solution to the matter, and that is one which is not available now. We feel that we must press through Congress an Enabling Act which will place federal authority over the registration and election officials in all the states and so make interference with, or prevention of, the proper execution of the election laws a federal offense. We had hoped to get this Enabling Act through Congress before its adjournment last spring but did not get farther than the introduction of the measure. We expect to be able to work for the passage of this Act at the coming session of Congress.

Very sincerely yours,
[Emma Wold]
Headquarters Secretary

So. That was it. There was nothin' they could do for me right now. I just had to be patient. She said, the next session of Congress. So maybe I would have to wait one year.

In the meantime, they promised to keep my name secret. So – I would keep my secret too. I wouldn't tell nobody about these letters until those ladies got it taken care of. If anybody can get it done, Miss Alice Paul can.

I just had to wait. So that's what I did.

(Folds letters and
puts them in the desk

drawer under
papers.)

Meantime, lots was goin' on in Southport to keep me busy.
You see, we were buildin' a new school for the colored
children in town. It was a Rosenwald school. That's Mr.
Julius Rosenwald from up north in Chicago, Illinois. He
was a rich man, and he was donatin' money to help us
build the school. We had been workin' all year to raise
money to build it. Most of the money we raised came from
the colored folk in the county, but some of the white folk
contributed money too. And the school district gave us
money as well.

I gave some of my money to help. This here school would
be the only colored school in all of Brunswick County that
went above the 8th grade. I was so excited. Little Baby
was goin' to be able to go to a real school and get a good
education!

But then, in January of 1921, just a few days before
classes were supposed to commence, we woke up to a
terrible commotion. Folks were shoutin' and runnin'
around. And the sky smelled of smoke. I ran to the door
and called out *What's wrong? What's wrong?*

I couldn't believe what they hollered back. *It's the school!
The new school! It done burned right to the ground!*

> (She stops talking. She
> wraps her arms around herself
> and rocks back and forth,

moaning/humming desperately
to herself. Whispers – *Look
what happened in Wilmington.*
After a moment, she stops
humming and runs to her desk.
She pulls out the envelopes
with the letters from the
women in Washington. She
stares at them, then looks for
a place to hide them. After
trying a couple of hiding
places, she pulls them back
out and rips them up, and
throws them away. After a
moment, she regains her
composure and turns back to
the audience. Her voice is
somber.)

It took a while after that to start to feel hopeful again.
Folks were pretty discouraged. But after a while, we
started collectin' money to build another school. We
collected even more money than the first time.

Just like the first time, the money came from all of
Brunswick County – colored folk, white folk, and the
school board. And the folks over at the Rosenwald
Foundation were real understandin' about the situation.
This time we had enough money to build a six–teacher
school instead of a four–teacher school. It took us four
years to do it, but finally, in 1925, the school was finished.
And this time, it didn't burn.

By then, Little Baby was 12 years old. If it hadn't been for that new school – called Brunswick County Trainin' School – that would have been just about the end of her education. But with the new school, she was able to go for several more years and get her high school diploma. She was a good student too. Real smart. And a hard worker. I was so proud.

So, Little Baby is all grown up. Nowadays, she calls herself Louise.

(Picks up her photo
from the desk.)

She's the only one I write letters to these days. See, she got married and moved away from here. She married herself a soldier. His name's Walter Dooley. He's a good man. And smart, like her. He fought in WWII and then in Korea. Then they sent him to Fort Bliss, in El Paso, Texas. That's where they live now.

(Shows her photo
to her guests.)

She works as a librarian, which is the perfect job for her because she always loved to read.

She writes such nice letters. She tells me all about her job and her pretty house and her friends. She collects baby dolls. She keeps them on shelves all over her house – can you imagine?

She likes to go out to eat in restaurants, and she loves to go to the theater and see plays. She has a good life. A real good life. My Little Baby.

Oh, Mama and Papa would be so proud.

> (Takes off her apron. Sits back down in the rocking chair. Any strength she had temporarily regained, is gone. She is feeling all of her years. She resumes a steady rocking.)

And so here I am. Still in Southport. Still waitin'. Still holdin' on to my secret.

Except – now I've told you. So, I guess it's not a secret no more.

Thirty-six years ago, I wrote those letters because I wanted so bad to vote. I wanted so much for my voice to be heard. For the longest time, I felt bad because I thought I had failed – because nothin' ever came of my letter writin'. After spendin' my whole life waitin', I'm still goin' to go to my grave without never bein' able to vote.

But now, after tellin' you my secret, I reckon I see things kind of different than I did before. I reckon those letters I wrote, they weren't for nothin' after all. You see, they were my way of protestin'. My way of standin' up for my rights. My way of bein' one of Miss Alice's Suffragists.

So, I'm glad I told you my secret. You can go ahead and tell whoever else you want. In fact, I hope you do. That way, even though I never got my chance to vote, my voice will still get heard.

Mama and Papa would be so proud.

(CURTAIN)

(END OF PLAY)

Reading Group Discussion Guide

1. Annie's parents, Allen and Martha (Evans) Clemmons were born into slavery in Brunswick County before the Civil War. Annie describes several limitations placed on her parents, such as laws that prohibited enslaved people from learning to read or getting married. They also lived under the constant concern that their family members might be taken away from them and sold, never to be seen again. Were any of these aspects of slavery a surprise to you? What do you think were the reasons for these laws?

2. Annie and the other members of the Southport Black community lived in the shadow of Wilmington, the largest city in North Carolina at that time. How did the progress made by Black Wilmingtonians make them feel? How did the subsequent backlash affect them?

3. What were some of the values passed down from Allen and Martha Clemmons to their daughter, Annie, and then on to her daughter, Maggie Louise? How do you think those values helped each generation achieve more success?

4. Being a free citizen of the United States was a point of pride for Annie's father and his children. What are some of the ways that family members demonstrated their citizenship and their dedication to Southport and to the United States? In what ways did the community accept their contributions? In what ways were they rebuffed?

5. In 1920, Annie Clemmons was a thirty-year-old working-class Black woman living in a small North Carolina fishing village of fewer than 1700 people. What do you think gave Annie the confidence to write a letter to the National Woman's Party in Washington, DC?

6. Annie took her secret efforts to vote to her grave. None of her extended family members in Southport knew about her correspondence with the National Woman's Party until the Southport Historical Society unearthed it in 2019. The play speculates about some reasons Annie might have kept her secret. What do you think her motives were?

7. Were you surprised to learn that some U. S. citizens were unable to vote until the mid-1900s? In what ways does Annie's story make you reflect on your own views on voting?

8. What will you remember most about Annie's story and about the history of Southport?

Frequently Asked Questions about the Life of Annie Clemmons

How did the Clemmons family come to live in Southport?

Both Annie's mother, Martha Evans, and her father, Allen Clemmons, were born into slavery in Brunswick County. Martha, who was seven years old when the Civil War ended, lived in Smithville with her mother Mary Moore. They were enslaved by Rev. W.M.D. Moore, minister of the Methodist Church.[1] Annie's father, Allen, who was a few years older than Martha, lived with his mother, Emma Caison, on a large farm in Lockwood's' Folly which was owned by Edward Clemmons.[2]

Life was hard for everyone in Smithville in those days, but especially hard for the formerly enslaved. Martha's mother, Mary, did what she could to provide for her three children, most likely by doing domestic work and taking in laundry. She sometimes turned to the Freedmen's Bureau to obtain rations of pork and corn meal to feed her family.[3] Other times, the family subsisted on what they could scavenge such as berries and honey.

It's likely that when she was growing up Martha was friends with a little boy named Frank Gordon. Frank was nine years old when the war ended. He, his mother, and his brothers and sisters had been living on the Swain plantation, a couple of miles outside of Smithville.[4] Following the war, they made their way to Smithville where they hoped for better opportunities.

Frank's mother, like Martha's, did her best to find work and feed her children. Frank and his siblings collected scrap iron, rags, and other junk to sell to a local scrap dealer to help feed the family. When they didn't have money to buy food, the children ate mulberries for lunch.[5] It's likely Martha and her siblings did much the same.

The children attended school whenever they could. Before the war, education had been illegal for Black people in North Carolina, freed or enslaved.[6] Both Frank and Mary's mothers wanted their children to learn to read and write so they'd have more opportunities and be less likely to be taken advantage of in the world.

Following the war's end, a Freedmen's school was established in St. Philip's Episcopal Church and at Trinity Methodist Church.[7] The teachers were schoolma'ams from a New England mission. The Black community soon formed their own school, led by AME missionary ministers within the newly established Methodist Episcopal Church for the Colored, which would eventually become St. James AMEZ Church.[8]

In December 1867, the church's trustees purchased a piece of land on the corner of Rhett Street and E. West Street.[9] In 1871, they obtained a structure that had once been part of the old federal quarantine hospital at Deep Water Point.[10] They moved it to the lot, forming the foundation of their first church.

An early minister, Rev. Abram G. Smith, and an assistant minister, Solomon C. Smith, became teachers to children and adults. In 1867, Abram had seventeen students and Solomon had eighteen. Two of their students were likely Martha Evans and Frank Gordon.[11]

Meanwhile, Allen Clemmons was living on a large farm in Lockwood's Folly. It's likely in the first few years following the war he continued to do farmwork. Because of his rural location, he didn't have much access to an education. Eventually, Allen made the difficult decision to leave his mother and the only home he had ever known.

Allen made his way to the town of Smithville, the only incorporated town in Brunswick County. At that time, eight hundred people were living in the town of Smithville, about a third of whom had once been enslaved.[12]

Moving to Smithville made all the difference in Allen's life. He found a good job working on a dredge boat on the Cape Fear River. Just as importantly, he found a strong faith-based community. The men he met in the congregation of the Methodist Episcopal Church were interested in politics and education as well as religion. Church members actively worked to improve their community.

It was through this church community that Allen met Martha. Before long, the two fell in love. On November 28, 1874, when Allen was twenty-one and Martha was sixteen, they were wed.[13]

Allen and Martha would have cherished the piece of paper that declared them legally to be husband and wife. Just a decade earlier, so much of the life they were now living would have been beyond imagination. Enslaved individuals had been barred from learning to read, forming churches, holding jobs, or getting married.

Soon, the couple would achieve another milestone. It was something their own parents and grandparents had only been able to dream of. Allen and Martha would start a family, secure in the knowledge that no one could ever take their children and sell them away from them.

Elizabeth Stanford Fuller, PhD

How did Allen Clemmons support his family?

Annie's father, Allen Clemmons, was a Civil employee for the United States Corps of Engineers. He worked on a dredge boat, removing excess silt and sand from the riverbed to maintain an adequate depth and navigability. He made $1.25 a day, working ten-hour shifts.[14]

After about twenty years working for the U.S. Dept. of Engineering, Allen was assigned to the new U.S.E. Dredge *Cape Fear*. This boat cost $60,000 when she was built in 1895. She had a hopper capacity of three hundred yards, meaning she could dredge up three hundred yards of silt in her storage hopper before unloading it outside the channel.[15]

By 1903, Allen had worked his way up to being a watchman with an annual salary of $420. He earned the same salary as the stokers, who fed the furnace, but less than the engineers. At that time, the lowest-paid employee on the dredge was Allen's 18-year-old son, Israel, who earned $180 per year working as a waiter. The highest-paid position was for the ship's Master, who earned $1500 annually.[16]

Allen Clemmons worked on the U.S.E. Dredge *Cape Fear* for the rest of his life. In 1922, the same year that Allen passed away, the *Cape*

Fear was retired, replaced by a newer steel hull, oil-burning dredge named *Comstock.*[17]

Allen's brother-in-law and next-door neighbor, Dan Lee, also worked for the U.S. Engineers. He was assigned to the snag boat *Gen. H. G. Wright* and was paid $1.25 per day as a general laborer. Snag boats removed dead trees, branches, and other similar debris from the water to help maintain the navigability of the Cape Fear River.[18]

Figure 1 The Crew of the U.S. Engineers Dredge Cape Fear circa 1914.

Not all of the men can be identified, but those that can are: Front row left to right, seated, John Eriksen, (unknown), Phil Fulcher, Kit McKeithan, Curtis Willis; second row, seated, (first two unknown), Willie Guthrie, (next two unknown), Johnnie McKeithan, James Grissom; third row, standing, Frank Greer, (next two unknown), Shuford Lewis, Dave Lewis, Capt. Lund, man back of Capt. Lund, Henry Van Tharp, and Capt. George Greer. Allen Clemmons is not identified in this photo. He may be in the back row where it appears there are a few unidentified Black men. Photo credit: Mrs. Esther Eriksen via the State Port Pilot.[19]

Where did the Clemmons family live?

Early in their marriage, Allen and Martha rented a home in Smithville on Caswell Street. In 1879, their first son, Allen Jr., was born in this home. They continued to live there until their son was four years old.[20]

In 1882 at the age of twenty-nine, Allen bought a home lot from Lewis and Henrietta Galloway. Lewis was the local postmaster. He sold the property to Allen for $50 cash, which equaled seven weeks' wages.[21]

The lot sat on the corner of E. Brown Street and Howe Street. It was in the newer part of town which had been annexed by the city in 1870. Smithville's original limits were composed of one hundred lots that had been surveyed and established at the town's founding in 1792. Eighty years later, the town was bursting at its seams. Since the river prevented the town from extending to the south, the borders were extended in every other direction, west, north, and east, spreading out in the shape of a fan.

For the most part, Black citizens couldn't purchase land within Smithville's original town limits. A few exceptions occurred along the eastern edge of town near the burying ground. However, Black citizens were able to purchase property in the newer section of town which started on the north side of Brown Street and extended about half a mile.

Investors such as Dr. O.F. Swasey from Massachusetts and L. A. Galloway were willing to sell property to the rising Black community. Much of this area, which was centered on the west side of Howe Street, became a neighborhood for Smithville's Black community. It was commonly referred to as "the West Side".

The lot that Allen Clemmons bought was 66 feet wide and 166 feet deep. This was twice as wide as many of the lots on the West Side.

Homeowners of the narrower lots tended to build shotgun houses that fit within the narrow width of their lots. The rooms in these houses were arranged in a single file, extending from the front to the back. It was said that when all the doors in the house stood open, a person could fire a shotgun clear through the house from the front door all the way out the back.

Since the Clemmons had a wider lot, it's likely they built a house in a style known as a "double cottage". This floorplan consists of two rooms on either side of a central passageway. It was a folk style of architecture that was common in Smithville from the colonial days through the 19th century, especially in the Black community.

The front door would have been positioned in the center of the house, with identical windows on either side. With no electricity in the home, the front porch would have provided a comfortable sitting area allowing the family to enjoy Smithville's sunshine and breezes while visiting with neighbors.

The privy would have been detached and built as far as possible from the main house. Like many houses in the Black community, the Clemmons house did not have a fireplace. Instead, they would have relied on a less expensive wood-burning stove for heating and cooking.

Allen was twenty-nine years old when he purchased his home on E. Brown Street. It would prove to be a wise investment as well as a secure home for his wife and nine children. Allen and Martha lived in their home until their deaths, Martha at sixty-one and Allen three years later at the age of sixty-nine.

Allen Clemmons left a will to his estate, which was uncommon for a Black man at that time. In his will, he divided the Brown Street property, leaving half to Annie and half to his youngest son, John. Annie inherited the portion that included the family home.[22] She continued to live there with her daughter, Louise. John erected his own residence on the other half.

Allen Clemmons owned additional property besides the family home. In 1895, at the age of forty-two, he acquired ten acres of farmland for $350 in an area known as the Savannah Plantation.[23] Over time, he expanded his holdings to include an adjoining fifty acres. This substantial sixty-acre tract of farmland was situated in a predominantly Black area along N.C. 87, in an unincorporated section of Smithville Township. Allen used this property for farming and raising livestock.

Allen's will did not specifically mention his farm property, leading to its designation as "heirs property" which was collectively bestowed upon all of his descendants. For over a century, Allen's heirs upheld ownership of the land, preserving it as a lasting legacy of Allen's life and work.[24]

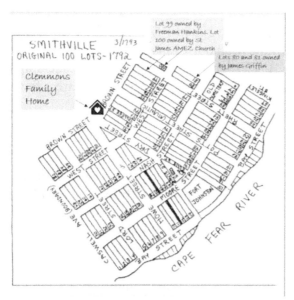

Figure 2 Map of the original 100 lots in Smithville. The Clemmons home is at the edge of the original town. Freeman Hankins a local Black builder purchased lot 99 and James Griffin a local Black investor purchased lots 80 and 81 across from the town's original burying ground. Lot 100 was purchased by a group of Black Southport men who then sold it in 1865 to the Colored Methodist Episcopal Church (later St. James AMEZ) Source: Southport Historical Society Archives.

Did Allen Clemmons and other Black men in Smithville vote?

Allen Clemmons came of voting age in 1874 when he was living in Smithville. As a member of the Methodist Episcopal Church, Allen was familiar with many of the Black men who were providing leadership to Smithville's burgeoning Black community. The following are a few of those early leaders.

William Brown (1805 – 1901)

William Brown, one of the trustees of the church, was also the first Black man elected to public office in Smithville. Brown, who had been a free man in Brunswick County for at least thirty years was also the most financially successful Black man in Smithville Township. In 1868, at the age of sixty-three, Brown was elected County Coroner. He was re-elected to a second term in 1870.[25]

Brown, a revered elder in the church, likely imparted wisdom and guidance to young church members such as Allen Clemmons, who showed an interest in furthering Smithville Township's Black community. These younger men who had still been children during the war, appeared to have formed a close-knit community. In the ensuing years, they pursued schooling, secured jobs, and formed families. They understood that the opportunities being presented to their generation were unprecedented. With youthful energy and determination, they worked to build a new society for their families and for the generations to come.

Whitfield Griffin (1848 – 1925)

One of these young men was Whitfield Griffin. In 1874 he was a twenty-six-year-old, married father of three who was also supporting his mother-in-law.[26] Griffin saw a need in the Black community for a cemetery where they could bury their loved ones. Smithville's existing burying ground was for White citizens only.

Before the war, enslaved individuals were buried in distant corners of plantations, typically in less productive land areas that were unsuitable for crops. Burials were hurried affairs that most often occurred at night so as not to interrupt the workday. Because graves were poorly marked, it was challenging for families to locate and visit them. In many cases, when family members were sold, they lost contact, never knowing when or where their loved one had passed.

Whitfield and Marietta (Smith) Griffin, along with their friend Henry Hankins, owned a two-acre property on the outskirts of Smithville. In 1874, a man named John N. Smith, possibly a relative of Marietta, was buried on that land. Two years later, a second grave for Kittie Smith, possibly another relative, was placed nearby.

In 1880, the Griffins and Hankins decided to sell the property to the trustees of the Methodist Episcopal Church (St. James AMEZ) to be used as a cemetery. As the population grew, more Black churches were established, and the cemetery came under the management of a committee representing all five of the Township's Black churches.[27]

The establishment of this burial ground, which became known as the John N. Smith Cemetery, allowed for daytime burials where funerals could last for as long as the mourners desired. Eventually, family plots were established, allowing relatives to be interred together. Family members could visit regularly and care for the graves. The community's cemetery provided comfort and peace of mind. Its existence embodied a deeply personal and significant aspect of freedom.

Solomon C. Smith (1843 – unknown)

Although younger than the church trustees, Solomon C. Smith played a prominent leadership role within the church. It's unclear how he came to live in Smithville, but by 1867, when he was twenty-three-years-old, he was teaching children at the newly established Methodist Episcopal church and acting as a part-time or assistant minister.

In 1868, Smith was one of the first Black members of the Board of Registration, traveling with B. D. Morrill to register voters in Lockwood's Folly, Town Creek, and Northwest.[28] By 1870, he was a husband and father and was working as the town's jailer while continuing his involvement in the church.[29]

Anthony Davis (1844-1893)

In 1874, Anthony Davis, 30, was married, and the father of five young children. Like Allen Clemmons, he worked as a boatman for the Federal government. Davis was a member of Pythagoras Lodge#6, Prince Hall Free and Accepted Masons which had been established in 1871. This organization fostered racial uplift, mutual aid, and social justice. Davis eventually became a Master Mason.[30]

In 1893, when Anthony Davis passed away, it was very unusual for the deaths of Black men to be mentioned in the newspaper, especially by name. But in Davis' case, the Southport Leader gave notice of his memorial service and described him as a sober, honest, and industrious man. The service was held at the Brunswick County Courthouse by the Pythagoras Lodge of Masons. It was described as being of a very impressive character. Several prominent Black men from Wilmington came down to attend the service.[31]

Although Davis died at the relatively young age of 49, he left a lasting legacy. His son, John R. Davis, became minister of the Methodist Episcopal church which had been renamed St. James

African Methodist Episcopal Zion (AMEZ) Church. Davis' grandson, Elmer Davis, served as an Executive Member of the Smithville Colored Citizens League that worked to improve public education for Smithville's Black students.[32]

Allen Clemmons (1853- 1922)

In 1874, Allen was twenty-one years old, married, and working on a government dredge boat. In addition to his participation in the church community, Allen became a member of Pythagoras Masonic Lodge#6, Prince Hall Masons.[33]Allen was one of the younger men in the group and was just beginning to explore how he could contribute to the community.

As the years went on, Allen chose not to take a leadership position within the Republican party. Perhaps he was not comfortable with public speaking. However, he did serve on the education committee for the Black Smithville public schools.[34] It's likely his desire to ensure that his children receive a good education, helped him overcome any reluctance he felt in taking on a leadership role.

Frank Davis (1854- 1925)

Frank Davis was twenty years old in 1874, just about the same age as Allen Clemmons. He was living at home with his mother and sister. Unlike the other men in his circle, Frank waited to get married until he was older. It wasn't until 1891 when he was 36 years old that he married Lydia Griffin, thirteen years his junior.[35]

Perhaps because he married later, Frank had more of an opportunity to get an education which gave him some unique opportunities. In 1892, Frank became Southport's first Black postmaster, serving for about a year.[36]

Frank was interested in local politics, attending local Republican meetings, and sometimes serving as secretary.[37] In 1896 he was nominated to run for Justice of the Peace by the Republican party.[38]

Franklin H. Gordon (1856 – 1939)

Frank Gordon was two years younger than Allen Clemmons, making him the youngest of the group. However, he was also one of the best educated because he had had more time for schooling. Frank was passionate about education for himself and for the entire Black community.

He contributed a great deal to the future of the community by becoming a teacher. His career spanned more than fifty years, during which time he taught hundreds of Black Brunswick County children to read.

In 1879, when he was twenty-three, Frank married eighteen-year-old Nannie Freeman. Frank's minister and former teacher, Rev. Solomon C. Smith performed the ceremony in Smith's home. Afterward, the couple moved next door to fellow church members, Anthony Davis and his family.[39]

Like many of the men in his social circle, Frank was active in local politics. In September 1886, a Republican party meeting was held in Smithville. William Brown, then eighty-one, acted as President, and Frank was secretary. During the meeting, Frank was selected to be one of the three delegates sent to the county convention.[40]

Frank passed away in 1939 at the age of 83, the last of that original post-war group of young men who were intent on improving their corner of the world. He continued to work for the betterment of his community right up until the end.

When Frank passed away the State Port Pilot put his picture and obituary in a place of honor, at the top of the front page. They praised his years of service as a teacher and described him as one of the most highly respected Black residents of Brunswick County. Both Black and White members of the community attended his funeral at St. James AMEZ church.[41]

Figure 3 Frank Gordon, Brunswick County Educator. Photo Courtesy Gordon Family.

The Election of 1874

The election of 1874 was a particularly exciting one for Smithville's Black community. It was the first time that a Black man was running for mayor of Smithville. It was even more exciting for Allen Clemmons and his friends because the candidate was their friend and minister, Rev. Solomon C. Smith.

Running against Smith on the conservative Democratic ticket was 64-year-old Captain Samuel B. Price. Captain Price was a popular steamship captain and a lifelong resident of Smithville. [42]

Allen and his friends certainly did all they could to help Smith get elected. Frank Gordon was still too young to vote, but Allen was

61

twenty-one and participating in his first election. He was likely extra excited to be able to vote for someone he knew.

But despite their best efforts, when the votes were tallied, Smith did not win. He did make a strong showing, coming within twenty-five votes of becoming Smithville's first Black mayor.[43]

A few months later, undaunted by his defeat for mayor of Smithville, Solomon Smith threw his hat in the ring for County Commissioner. At that same time, William Brown was running for his third term as County Coroner. However, neither man won. Across the county and the state, the conservative party was taking back control of North Carolina's government.[44]

Both men continued to stay involved with the Republican party. In 1876, they were both delegates to the County Convention, with Whitfield Griffin serving as one of the alternatives.[45]

The Election of 1887

The election of 1887 stands out in Southport's history. Although the names of everyone involved aren't known, the men already mentioned were likely active participants.

The election took place about ten years after the end of Reconstruction. In many Southern states, Black participation in elections was diminished or non-existent due to voter suppression laws and violent intimidation. But in North Carolina, Black voter participation remained strong. So, it was a surprise on Election Day in 1887 when Black voters didn't appear at the polls.

All day long, the White voters came to the polls and submitted their votes. Due to different colored ballots and glass voting boxes, it was easy to see which way each man voted. Some men enjoyed loitering around the polls and keeping an informal tally of which candidates were winning. Votes were pretty evenly split between the two parties.

On this particular day, the polls were near closing when a group of Black men made their way to the polls. One by one each man cast his vote for their candidates. The result was a resounding victory for Republican J.L. Wescott as mayor. But the big surprise was for town commissioners. J.A. Bell, a White Republican, and four Black men were the winners! They were the first Black aldermen in Southport's history.

Newspaper reports indicate that "the White faction were dumbfounded and the community was disgusted by the result". Presumably, they meant the White community, because the members of the Black community were pretty pleased with themselves. They had reminded both parties that they wielded a great deal of political power and their votes should not be taken for granted.[46]

The Election of 1898

This statewide election was the most divisive in North Carolina's history. The conservative Democratic party waged a months-long White Supremacy campaign to encourage and coerce White Populist and Republican voters to give up their alliance with the predominantly Black Republican Party and return to the party of the White man.[47]

The result, which was accomplished "by hook or by crook" was a sweeping landslide for the Democratic Party. Voter intimidation and ballot stuffing were two of the tactics used to influence the outcome. In Southport, conservative canvassers discarded the Republican and Populist ballots because they had been printed on the wrong color of paper. [48]

The Democrats capitalized on their victory and maintained control of North Carolina governance for sixty years before the state began to switch to a Republican majority. This change could never have been imagined in 1867 when the fledgling party held its first meeting of the North Carolina Republicans in Raleigh.

But by the 1960s, both the Democrat and Republican Party platforms had undergone substantial changes. Democrats had implemented influential programs that were increasingly unpopular in the South such as Roosevelt's New Deal, Truman's military integration, and Johnson's Great Society initiatives, including landmark legislation like the Civil Rights Act of 1964 and the Voting Rights Act of 1965. Concurrently, the Republican Party had continued to shift towards a more socially conservative stance. This simultaneous ideological shift prompted North Carolina and the wider South to switch their allegiance to the Republican Party where it has remained to the present day.

The Election of 1900

The election of 1900 continued the work begun in the election of 1898 to secure the state for the conservative Democratic party. It would also be the last election in which Allen Clemmons and his circle of friends were able to vote. On the ballot was a Suffrage Amendment which would have been more accurately named the Disenfranchisement Amendment. This proposed amendment required all Black voters to take a literacy test and to pay a poll tax in order to vote. The amendment passed by a wide margin in the state, although Brunswick County voted it down by 143 votes.[49]

Like many Black men of his generation, Allen Clemmons had never learned to read so under the new law he lost his right to vote due to a lack of literacy. All his life he had been too busy working and supporting his family to attend school. First, he had supported his mother and then his wife and children. But as it turned out, it wouldn't have mattered anyway.

Allen's friend, Frank Gordon, was a teacher. He could read and write so well that he taught school all over Brunswick County. Yet when he went to register, he was turned away by the registrar just like Allen had been. The same was true for all of Allen's sons, who had gone to school and learned to read and write.

Toward the end of his life, Allen Clemmons finally learned to read and write. Perhaps Annie, who had started out as a teacher, was the one who taught him. It's likely Allen wanted to be ready. If the registrar ever started administering the test fairly, he'd be able to pass and regain his right to vote. Instead, Allen never again participated in another election. It was a demoralizing defeat for a man who spent forty years working for the federal government and who was so proud to be a citizen that he selected July 4th as his own birthday.

Figure 4 Allen Clemmons. Photo courtesy of the Clemmons Family

What was Annie's life like as a child in Southport?

Annie's childhood was very different from the ones her parents had experienced. She and her siblings were part of the first generation to have never known slavery or the destitution that followed during reconstruction.

She was the sixth surviving child born into her family and the second girl. By the time she was ten years old, she would have three younger brothers, at which point her family was complete.[50]

The entire family lived together in their own little house. She was raised by both of her parents and she didn't have to worry about any of her family being sold away from her.

Likely, everyone in the family worked as soon as they were able. All the money they earned went toward the support of the family.[51] In all the years that Annie was growing up, she never had to go hungry or wonder where her next meal was coming from.

When she was young, Annie stayed at home and helped her mother with the babies and the household chores. By the time she was ten, she started school where she eagerly learned reading, writing, and arithmetic.

Annie's neighborhood was a close-knit community. Her neighborhood was filled with family and friends including her uncle

Dan Lee and his family who lived next door. Everyone worked and played together, with the adults keeping an eye on all of the children.

On Sundays, Annie's family walked a few blocks to St. James African Methodist Episcopal Zion (AMEZ) Church. She attended church services and Sunday school.

Perhaps in the evenings or over the supper table, Annie's parents would share stories of the way things used to be before the war. But like any child, her parents' childhood seemed far removed from her own life. She never experienced those hardships firsthand, which likely contributed to the sense of confidence and self-worth that she carried throughout her life.

Annie was part of a new generation, and the town she was growing up in was very different from the one her parents talked about. Even the name of the town had changed from Smithville to Southport. And the community had expanded. Smithville township had grown to about 2,500 citizens, nearly half of whom were Black.[52]

By the early 1900s, there were five Black churches, two one-room elementary schools, a Prince Hall Masonic Lodge, a Royal Knight's Lodge, and a 2.5-acre Black cemetery. While the majority of Black men worked as unskilled laborers and Black women as laundresses, there were also fishermen, seamen, preachers, farmers and teachers.[53]

In 1900, the literacy rate among Black adults in Southport rose from a mere five percent in 1870 to approximately fifty-six percent. This significant increase was due to the resolute commitment of Black citizens to obtain an education, supported by the devoted efforts of educators such as Mr. Frank Gordon. Mr. Gordon dedicated an impressive fifty-five years of his life to teaching, contributing significantly to this positive shift in literacy rates that surpassed the state average.[54]

Another devoted educator was Miss Sarah McKenzie Moore who was approximately sixteen years younger than Frank Gordon. Sarah held the distinction of being the first Black person in Southport to obtain a four-year high school education.[55]

Since Brunswick County was still decades away from establishing a Black high school, Sarah had to attend a boarding school to pursue her education. She traveled two hundred and fifty miles up the Atlantic coast to Elizabeth City, where she enrolled in the high school program at the State Colored Normal School.[56]

A few years after she graduated, Sarah got a job as a teacher at Pine Level School out on River Road. She went on to have a forty-five-year career as a teacher at various schools around the county. In 1942, at the age of sixty-three, Sarah achieved another first. She became the first person in Brunswick County to retire under the State's retirement system.[57]

Like the Clemmons, the Gordons, and the McKenzies, nearly half of local Black families owned their own homes in 1900. Dan Lee, Whitfield Griffin, James Griffin, Henry Hankins, Freeman Hankins, Malissa Jackson, and Abram Galloway were just a few of the one-hundred-twelve Black homeowners in Smithville Township.[58]

Despite this progress, Southport was still just a small fishing village, existing in the shadow of Wilmington, the largest and most important city in North Carolina. Tons of cotton were shipped out of its port, and international goods were shipped in. Wilmington's railroad connected to all points north and west, enabling it to support the state's international commerce. Southport simply couldn't provide the employment opportunities that were available there.

Wilmington's population of 25,000 people was ten times larger than all of Smithville Township. The city had had a majority Black population since before the Civil War. Enslaved workers had been the city's stevedores, ship crews, builders, and craftsmen. Many continued to do the same jobs after they were freed.

Following the war, the Black population continued to grow, as emancipated Black men and women from neighboring counties were drawn to Wilmington and its potential for upward mobility.[59]

One in five of all businesses in Wilmington had Black owners. Black proprietors owned ten out of eleven of the restaurants and twenty out of twenty-two of the barbershops. A partnership of two Black men owned one of the four fish-and-oyster shippers in Wilmington.

Black men were the most sought-after craftsmen. While enslaved, many had performed skilled labor. Once they were emancipated, they were able to use those skills to support themselves and their families. Consequently, they were the tailors, the blacksmiths, the shoemakers, the stonemasons, the plasterers, the plumbers, the wheelwrights, the brick masons, and the carpenters.

There was a small but significant Black middle class growing up in Wilmington. There were Black lawyers, architects, builders, teachers, and principals. There were six Black school board members, four or five deputy sheriffs, fourteen policemen, two fire departments, a legislator, a registrar of deeds, several attorneys, postal workers, mail carriers, a coroner, and four health officers. And in 1898, three of Wilmington's ten aldermen were Black.

Most conspicuously, John Dancy, the collector of Customs for the Port, was Black. This well-paying federal job was appointed by the President and was the highest-paid government job in North Carolina, earning more than the Governor.

Like many Black citizens of Southport, it's likely the Clemmons talked often about Wilmington and the opportunity that would be available for their sons if they someday moved there. After hearing their conversations about the big city, little Annie probably dreamed of visiting someday and seeing the streetlights and electric trolleys.

By 1898, a forty-year focus on education by the Black residents of Wilmington had enabled them to have a high literacy rate. The city's Black reading audience was large enough to sustain what was possibly the only Black-owned daily newspaper in the country. This paper, The Daily Record, was read by both Black and White residents and was supported in part by advertisements from White businesses.[60]

In 1898, when Annie was eight years old, her childhood innocence was shattered. That was the year that the massacre occurred in Wilmington, just twenty-five miles upriver from her home.

Despite her young age, she would have heard about the terrible goings-on. News traveled down the Cape Fear River with the steamboats. Some survivors, fleeing the danger, made their way over land to the safety of Smithville where they recounted their ordeal.

The repercussions of the tragedy were felt downriver in Southport. Wilmington had always been a beacon of hope for the smaller Black community. But on that day in November 1898, all that little Annie Clemmons knew was that her world no longer felt safe.

The father she revered had been humiliated when his vote had been discarded as worthless. Her mother, who had once dreamed of the possibilities that awaited her sons, was now heartsick at the possibility of her children being gunned down in the streets.

After all of their hard work and all of their so-called progress, Allen and Martha realized that nothing they did could keep their family safe. It could all be gone in an instant.

It wasn't long after the massacre that Annie started school. It's evident she took her education seriously. Very likely her parents told her that her schooling was the one thing that no one could take from her. As long as she had an education and the ability to work hard, she could look out for herself. Beyond that, she would need to trust in the Lord that it would all work out for the best.

What was Annie's career like?

In 1908 when Annie came of age, career options for Black women were limited, especially in Southport. At the time, the three main occupations were laundress, teacher, and nurse. Annie had likely had enough of the sweltering, backbreaking work of doing laundry for her own family of seven brothers to want to make a career of it.

Her first choice of profession was teaching. She tried it for a few years but by the time she was twenty-one, she had turned to nursing. She trained under Dr. J. Arthur Dosher, a well-respected Southport surgeon, and it was here that she found her niche.

Dr. Dosher made house calls to visit his patients. Nurses and midwives supplemented his work, traveling to private homes to provide ongoing care and support.

In 1917, Dr. Dosher enlisted in the military and was sent overseas to France to serve in the army.[61] Consequently, he was away when the "Spanish flu" pandemic hit Southport in October 1918. Dr. D. I. Watson, who owned Smithville's pharmacy, and Dr. F. R. Brown were on hand to handle it.[62]

The doctors had had recent experience with an epidemic when measles broke out among the troops at Ft. Johnston.[63] Therefore, they were familiar with a protocol for protecting the community from the spread of disease.

Dr. Watson took a particularly strong leadership role, publishing a request in the newspaper to limit travel and business dealings between Southport and Wilmington during the outbreak.[64] Southport was quick to cancel schools, limit business hours, and encourage mask usage. This was likely done under Dr. Watson's advice.

Fort Caswell, which had over twelve hundred troops stationed there, was put under quarantine. No one was permitted in or out of the camp, and even the mail run from Wilmington was stopped.[65]

During this time Annie worked tirelessly to nurse the sick. There was no cure for the flu, so she focused on providing comfort and relieving the symptoms. She applied cool compresses, fresh air, and clean linens.

The only medicines at her disposal were aspirin and Vicks VapoRub which flew off the pharmacy shelves so quickly that it was hard to come by. Liquor was sometimes used to treat a cough, but Southport was a dry town. The only access was through Watson's pharmacy by prescription. Annie's more affluent patients were the only ones who could afford such luxuries. Annie likely resorted to folk remedies as well, such as leaving cut onions in the sickroom to absorb the illness.

The first wave of the pandemic in Southport lasted a little over a month. Annie provided her nursing services in houses all over town, in both the Black and White communities.

Southport was written up in the newspaper for having such a low fatality rate from the pandemic. Credit was given to Dr. Brown, but there's little doubt that a great deal of credit went to Annie and the other women who provided nursing services.[66]

While there had been plenty of sickness in Southport, including Dr. Watson himself, there were no fatalities within the city limits. There were at least two fatalities outside of town in the Black community, where the illness was exacerbated by poorer nutrition and less access to health care.[67]

In all, thirty-five people died in Brunswick County, considerably fewer than the 164 who died in New Hanover. More than five thousand people died of the flu in North Carolina in October 1918, the month that the first wave of the pandemic swept through the state. This was more than twice as many North Carolina soldiers who died in WWI.[68]

Despite Annie's exposure to the flu, neither she nor any of her family members died from it. Even her brother who was serving in the military where the flu was rampant, came through unscathed. This was made more remarkable because the virus was known to be particularly hard on young adults in their prime.

Subsequent waves of the pandemic came back at least twice more during the following eighteen months, each mutation more deadly than the last. Annie stepped in to nurse the sick each time. After the crisis had passed, Annie received a certificate from the state, thanking her for her service.[69]

Just as the Wilmington massacre was a defining moment in Annie's childhood, the flu pandemic was a defining moment in her adulthood. Through it, she recognized her self-worth and her value to her community. It was just two years later that the 19th Amendment passed and Annie tried to register to vote. After all that Annie had done in service to her community, the rejection by the local registrar must have been an especially painful blow.

What was Annie like as a mother?

In 1913, at the age of twenty-three, Annie gave birth to a little girl.[70] She named her daughter Maggie Louise but everyone called her "Little Baby."[71] Annie never married and she never shared the identity of her baby's father or the circumstances of her baby's birth with anyone. Even then, Annie valued her privacy and knew how to keep a secret.

Annie didn't seem to mind not having a husband. She and Little Baby were a complete family by themselves. Annie worked hard to provide a good home for her baby. A year after her daughter's birth, Annie bought a small lot on Lord Street from Dr. O. F. Swasey of Massachusetts for $75. On it, she built a snug little cottage.[72]

Annie's cottage, along with other houses constructed by Southport's Black citizens, created a close-knit community of homes and small businesses. A little more than half of the Black families in Smithville Township owned their own homes in this area of Southport or outside of town in a community along Jabbertown Road.

Annie and her daughter resided in her Lord Street home for about five years, with her brother James and his wife Julia (Joyner) living next door. It was a short walk from her parents' house, three blocks south and one block east.

When her mother fell ill, Annie moved back home to care for her. After her mother's passing, she remained in her parents' home to look after her widowed father.

Annie raised her daughter with the same values with which she had been raised. She took her to church every week and surrounded her with family and community.

Annie worked hard to provide an education for her daughter. She was always a smart little girl who loved to read.[73] At that time, Southport's Black community was working with the Rosenwald Foundation to build a public school. It would be the only school in Brunswick County that went beyond eighth grade.

It's all but certain that Annie was involved in the planning and fundraising for the school. After some major setbacks, the school finally opened in 1925, in time for Louise to go to high school there.

Louise graduated from Brunswick County Training school in 1930.[74] During WWII she met and married a soldier and moved away from Southport. Although she visited her mother regularly, they never lived together again.

Annie loved her daughter fiercely and made many sacrifices for her while she was growing up. So, it was only natural for her to make a sacrifice once more for her daughter's well-being. She wanted her beloved Little Baby to have all the opportunities in life that she could, even if it meant leaving Southport and her family. So, Annie encouraged her daughter to follow her dreams wherever they took her.

Annie's daughter was likely a motivation for her own desire to vote. Little Baby was seven years old when the 19th Amendment was ratified. Annie wanted to have a voice in local politics to make life better for her daughter. She wanted to have an influence over how much money was spent on public education. Perhaps she hoped to reduce the segregation that kept her daughter from checking a book out from the library, sitting downstairs at the AMUZU movie theater, or having ice cream at the soda counter while waiting for a prescription to be filled at the drugstore.

Annie held strong memories of her father walking to town to vote in elections, pride evident in his every step. She cherished a vision that she kept close to her heart: she wanted her daughter to witness her journey to the courthouse to exercise her own right to vote.

Annie desperately wanted her daughter to know that in the United States of America regardless of whether you were Black, or a woman, or financially challenged, you still had a right to vote. She wanted to instill in her daughter the belief that every vote mattered, and every voice deserved to be heard, including her own.

Unfortunately for Annie, the Brunswick County registrar didn't agree.

Elizabeth Stanford Fuller, PhD

What was the reaction in Southport toward women voting?

The fight for U.S. women's right to vote had been going on since 1848 when the First Women's Rights Convention was held in Seneca Falls, New York. Since that time, progress had been agonizingly slow. When WWI broke out, many thought the movement should take a backseat to the war effort. But Alice Paul and the National Woman's Party (NWP) refused to slow their campaign. Despite members being arrested, thrown in jail, and physically abused they continued to protest and to publicly embarrass the government for fighting for democracy overseas while denying it to half its population at home.

Following WWI, views on women's suffrage began to shift. Countries like Canada, several European nations, and twenty U.S. states had already granted voting rights to women. The idea of a U.S. constitutional amendment was becoming more popular.

Finally, even Woodrow Wilson warmed to the idea. He gave a speech to congress urging them to pass the women's suffrage amendment.[75]

He said,

"We have made partners of the women in this war; shall we admit them only to a partnership of suffering and sacrifice and toil and not to a partnership of privilege, and right?"

- *Woodrow Wilson, Address to the Senate on the 19th Amendment. September 30, 1918*

On June 4, 1919, Congress passed the proposed 19th amendment and sent it to the states to be ratified. In less than a year thirty-five states approved it. Only one more was needed. The nation's eyes turned to North Carolina to see what it would do.

Across the state, newspapers were abuzz with news of the proposed amendment. Both the Raleigh News and Observer and the Wilmington Morning Star were in favor of its passage. But many politicians and members of the public were in doubt.

Naysayers claimed that giving women the vote would make them less feminine and would undermine the stability of marriages across the country. They were also concerned that women would use the vote to pass progressive laws that prohibited the sale of alcohol or limited the use of child labor.

Complicating matters in North Carolina and other Southern states was the concern over the voting rights of Black women. North Carolina had effectively shut down voting rights for Black men twenty years earlier. Some were concerned that if women were guaranteed the right to vote, then Black women would be able to vote as well, re-opening the door that they had so firmly closed twenty years before.[76]

Others took a more pragmatic approach. They believed that sooner or later Blacks would regain the vote. If White women were able to vote, they would help to outnumber Black votes.[77]

At that time, Southport did not have a newspaper, but Annie would likely have read all of the articles and editorials in the Wilmington newspapers. She may have also heard the issue discussed around town or in the homes of people that she nursed for.

She likely discussed what she learned with her brothers and her parents. Her brothers had all come of age in the 20th century after Black

North Carolina men had had their voting rights taken away. Did they wonder if perhaps it would be their sister who would have the first chance to vote?

Her parents would have vividly remembered the Massacre of 1898. Did they worry that this new amendment would lead to trouble?

Southport's White community debated the amendment as well. Women sitting at the kitchen table and men gathered at the whittler's bench all debated the implications of giving women the right to vote.

In June, Lola Trax from the Baltimore Division of Women Suffrage, along with representatives of the NC Equal Suffrage association and other local sympathizers, spoke at the County Courthouse in favor of the amendment. Men and women filled the hall until it was standing room only. Following the meeting, Mrs. R. W. Davis, wife of Southport's former mayor, was named head of the Brunswick County ratification committee. [78]

Meanwhile, the state legislature was preparing to decide on the proposed amendment. Governor Thomas W. Bickett, who was not personally in favor of its passage, reluctantly recommended that the Assembly move to pass it, saying,

> "I am profoundly convinced that it would be part of wisdom and grace for North Carolina to accept the inevitable and ratify the amendment."
>
> *-Thomas W. Bickett's address to the joint session of the* General *Assembly on August 13, 1920*

But, on August 17, 1920, North Carolina's state senate voted to postpone a decision on the amendment until the following year, knowing full well the matter would be settled before then. In fact, the very next day, Tennessee's legislature became the 36th state to ratify the amendment, making it the Nineteenth Amendment of the U.S. Constitution.

After the amendment's passage, Southport leadership actively supported its implementation. Southport Woman's Club partnered with Mayor J. W. Ruark to organize a lecture series aimed at educating women about their new civic duties.[79]

The initial citizenship lecture, held at the Army and Navy Club, drew a sizable audience of women and men. Mrs. Anna Miller Davis, the first woman to register to vote in Brunswick County, presided over the gathering and introduced the speakers. Mayor Ruark explained the registration laws and encouraged women to exercise their new privileges by registering and participating in voting.[80]

Other speakers discussed the importance of suffrage and the need for women to fulfill their new civic duty. Speakers came down from Wilmington to participate. To make it more enjoyable, musical performances were included in each class.[81]

The first few presentations were so popular that they decided to continue the lecture series for several weeks. They also appointed a committee of women to go door to door to each house in the community to encourage women to register.[82]

Annie Clemmons wasn't invited to the lecture series. It was for White women only. No one came to her door to encourage her or any of her friends and neighbors to register or learn more about their rights.

It was the same story all across the state. The specific circumstances varied by county in North Carolina, but most Black women were turned away by their local registrar. In Wilmington, approximately three thousand women registered to vote in 1920, nearly doubling the city's registered voters. Of those women who registered, only ten were Black.[83]

Elizabeth Stanford Fuller, PhD

What was Annie Clemmons' reaction to the 19th Amendment?

Annie did not receive the same information and support for registering to vote that the White women did. There were no classes, no lectures, no visitors, and no pamphlets teaching her about her civil rights and responsibilities.

It's possible Annie's sister and her friends thought she was crazy for even thinking about voting. It had been twenty years since Black men had been able to vote in North Carolina. How would a Black woman even begin to go about it? It's possible her father who still remembered the pride that he had felt when voting, was the only one who supported her dreams.

Annie had always kept her own counsel and done things her own way. She was an analytical woman who would have considered the matter clearly before she decided to register. It is almost possible to see her pondering the topic as she went about her workday.

As she trudged from house to house she might have worked her way through her list of reasons why she should be allowed to vote. With each step, she would recite another qualification. I am a property owner. I am a taxpayer. I am a churchgoer. I am a mother. I am a law-abiding citizen. My family has lived in Brunswick County for generations. Besides, who donated money and rolled bandages for the Red Cross during the war? Who served as a nurse in all the houses in Southport during the flu epidemic?

I did. That's who.

And so, Annie screwed up her courage, pressed her best clothes, and made her way to the courthouse to register.

Entering through the back door designated for Black citizens, she would have made her way to the registrar's office. It's likely he was prepared. As soon as the amendment had passed, he would have expected at least one Black woman to come to his office looking to register.

Annie took his literacy tests, reading and writing whatever parts of the Constitution he selected. Despite her obvious literacy, he turned her away for being unable to read and write well enough to suit him.

Shocked and disappointed, Annie had no one she could appeal to. She would have turned away, her face burning with embarrassment and shame, as she made her way out through the same back door through which she had come in.

It would only be later when she shared her experience with her family and a few trusted friends that she began to look at the situation differently. She discovered that no Black person in all of Brunswick County had been able to read and write well enough to suit the registrar.

The fault was not hers. It was his.

It wasn't long before Annie decided to find a way around the registrar. She recalled the articles she had read in the Wilmington newspaper about Miss Alice Paul and the National Woman's Party (NWP). Surely these women who had stood up to the President of the United States could help her stand up to the Brunswick County registrar.

Annie searched the article for Alice Paul's name and the name of the organization she ran. She wrote a letter which she mailed to Washington, DC.

Southport, NC
Oct. 10th 1920
The National Woman's Party- Washington D.C.

To The Sect. of above Party,

I am an american colored woman property owner in Brunswick County State of North Carolina and am seeking way to vote by mail if there is a way, because a colored person in my county is unable to vote, because they are colored. Please send me information how to send votes or register to general Headquarters by mail before it is too late to register.

am oblige.
(Miss) Anna A. Clemons
Bx 294   Southport N.C.[84]

Every day Annie would have gone to the post office, checking her PO Box for a response.

Finally, ten days after she mailed her letter a response came from Emma Wold, NWP secretary. Miss Wold informed her that there was no way to register by mail. It had to be done in person. She asked Annie to go to the courthouse and try to register and then to let them know what happened.

But Annie had already tried to register and had been rejected. Miss Wold had misunderstood. Annie had to make her understand her situation. She had to convince NWP that she was a serious person who understood her rights. She wouldn't have bothered them if she had not already done everything that she could to register.

Annie sat down to compose her thoughts. She likely wrote several practice letters until she got the words just how she liked them. She wanted her letter to sound as professional as possible. She even used the same formal greeting that Miss Wold had used in her letter. When she was satisfied, she copied it all over in her best handwriting.

Oct. 24th 1920

Miss Emma Wold: Washington, D.C

My Dear Miss Wold:

In reply to your letter, which was duly received yesterday, will take the greatest of pleasure to write you my result, in attempting or trying to register. I went before the registrar Oct 15th and was refused to be registered, as this board requires all colored to be able to read and write to "suit" the registrar, and all persons of colored origin in this whole county have been unable to suit the registrar; North Carolina laws require one to be able to read and write, to register, still we have in our county ones to fill requirements then they are refused.

I hope, and ask if you should have this matter investigated, then please do not let my name be brought into this matter because there is so much prejudice existing until I am most assured I will be a victim of lawless Mob.

To show you I am no agitator, or race leader, I will try to explain just my position. I am a nurse, have nursed in most every home in this town for past 9 years, acting at times as assistant to one of the South's best Surgeons Dr. J Arthur Dosher of this county. I donated to the Red Cross, volunteered during the epidemic of "1918," "flu," and hold a certificate for heroic services rendered over my State.

I own property, and pay my tax. I am a Christian. I belong to the Methodist Church. I attend to my own business, don't interfere with no race of people, and try to live here as I expect to live when I pass in the great beyond, that is in peace. I have seven (7) brothers, law-abiding, supposed to be citizens, denied the same as myself.

Hoping and resting assured you will not use my name in this matter that I will close.

From
Anna A. Clemons Bx 294   Southport N.C.

Annie read over her letter one last time. She hoped they would understand her predicament. She had tried to register and had been denied. What would the ladies at the National Woman's Party do next? Would they investigate? What if they wrote to the registrar? What if someone came down here? What if they used her name?

Finally, she took a deep breath and sealed the envelope. After affixing a stamp, she took it to the post office to mail. As her mama had told her years before, do all you can and then trust the Lord to make it come out alright.

For the next few weeks, Annie walked around with a knot in her stomach. She was jumpy and sometimes didn't hear when people were talking to her. Her mind was on her letter and that investigation.

Finally, she found a letter in her box at the post office. She quickly stuck it in her skirt pocket and carried it home. She wanted to read it in private.

When Annie finally read Mrs. Wold's letter, it's likely she felt both disappointment and relief. She was disappointed that they couldn't help her, but she was also relieved that they weren't going to do an investigation. Instead, they said they needed to pass another law. A law to make people follow the law.

Annie folded the letter and put it back in its envelope. She tucked both letters in a drawer of her desk. She'd done all she could. Now she just had to trust in the Lord and the ladies of the NWP to do the rest.

Was Annie right to be concerned about the threat of a lawless mob?

In Annie's letter to Emma Wold, secretary of the National Woman's Party, she implored them not to use her name out of fear of retribution. She wrote, "there is so much prejudice existing until I am most assured I will be a victim of lawless Mob". Was Annie being melodramatic or was she right to be concerned?

Annie wrote her letter in 1920, a period that is often considered the lowest point in U.S. race relations. The previous summer of 1919 is known as the Red Summer because hundreds of Black citizens were killed by mobs of White citizens in more than sixty American cities.[85]

In January 1920 the Tuskegee Institute published a tally of known lynchings in the previous year. There were eighty-two altogether, up from sixty-four the previous year. Seventy-seven of the lynchings had occurred in the South, including three in North Carolina. Seventy-five of the victims were Black, including one Black woman. The tally focused solely on individual murders rather than on community-wide violence. The means varied from hanging, burning, and shooting. The motivations for the lynchings ranged from murder (13) to alleged incendiary talk (2) and writing an improper letter (2).[86]

This report was printed on the front page of the Wilmington Morning Star, a newspaper that Annie was familiar with. She would have read this report and known that her correspondence with NWP was dangerous. It's likely her childhood memories of the Wilmington Massacre and the fear it had instilled in her family, would never have been far from her mind. She would have known that there was nowhere that was truly safe from this type of reprisal.

If Annie had any doubts about her imagination running away with her, they were shattered just three months later. In January 1921, the newly built Rosenwald school for Black students in Brunswick County burned to the ground before any classes could be held.[87]

The school had been the pride of the Brunswick County Black community. They had worked for several years and raised nearly $9,000 from the community and the Rosenwald foundation to fund it. The school would have been the first Black school in the county that would have gone beyond the eighth grade.[88]

No official explanation for the fire has been documented.

Figure 5 Brunswick County Training School#1, a Rosenwald School. This school burned to the ground January 1921 before any classes could be held. The building on the right is the previous Black school building, one of two in Southport ca. 1920. Southport Historical Society Archives.

What was Annie's life like in her later years?

Annie continued to work as a nurse all of her life. She owned a piece of farmland on Bell Swamp Rd. adjacent to her father's farm. After Louise was grown and had left Southport, Annie lived on the farm property by herself. In her final years, she returned to Southport and lived in the small house on E. Brown Street that she had inherited from her father.

Annie is remembered as a strong woman who lived life on her own terms. She traveled independently around Smithville Township, driving a wooden mule-cart. She was known to frequent backwoods where she would cut firewood and gather pine straw for resale.

Annie ignored the fashions of the time, preferring to dress in bib overalls and a flannel shirt.[89] It was easier to climb up and down in a cart and perform chores in these more practical, masculine clothes. Because her clothes were sturdy, they were less likely to get damaged while doing manual labor.

Her overalls had the added advantage of downplaying her femininity. A stranger passing her on the road might assume she was a man and leave her to her work. If he recognized she was a woman, she might not have been as lucky.

Not that Annie relied on luck to keep herself safe. Annie was known to carry a pistol wherever she went.[90] Her race and her gender made her doubly vulnerable to assault. Living alone and traveling along secluded back roads also increased her need to protect herself.

Since Annie closely guarded her privacy, there's no way to know whether she ever faced any dangerous circumstances. However, her reputation for always being prepared likely kept most men from even trying.

Annie was as protective of her property as she was of her person. In 1922, when a neighbor's livestock was continually trespassing on her land, she filed a lawsuit and won. The court awarded her $50 in damages, plus recovery of court costs.[91]

In 1956, Annie passed away from kidney disease. She was sixty-five. In her final days, her late sister's daughter, Inez Green Smith, helped care for her.[92]

Annie kept the secret of her correspondence with Miss Emma Wold of the National Woman's Party all her life. Perhaps she had hoped that one day the Enabling Act Miss Emma had promised her would pass. On that glorious day, she would tell her secret and share her letters.

But Annie died before that day could come. She died waiting for the law to pass, and for the federal government to take a stand. She died waiting for North Carolina to do the right thing and guarantee the right to vote to all its women and men.

Where is Annie's final resting place?

Anna Alene Clemmons is buried at the John N. Smith Cemetery in Southport, North Carolina. This is the same cemetery that was established in 1880, when Whitfield and Marietta Griffin and Henry Hankins sold the property to be used as a cemetery for the Black community in Smithville Township.

John N. Smith Cemetery is the largest extant Black cemetery in Brunswick County. Over 1,725 people are interred there, in both marked and unmarked graves. Thanks to the efforts of John N. Smith Restoration and Preservation, Inc., and the assistance of the Southport Historical Society, the cemetery is listed on the National Register of Historic Places.

Annie is buried in a family plot near her parents and several of her siblings. Her daughter is not buried there but she did purchase a marker for Annie's grave that reads "My Beloved Mother, Rest In Peace, Gone But Not Forgotten."

In 2024, the Southport Historical Society in conjunction with John N. Smith Cemetery Restoration and Preservation, Inc., Ricky Evans Gallery, and the City of Southport, created and installed a historical marker commemorating Annie's life. The marker displays copies of her correspondence with the National Woman's Party. Annie's original letters are stored in the NWP archives in the U.S. Library of Congress.

Figure 6 Annie Clemmons' grave is nestled among the graves of her mother, father, and other family members. Her marker was chosen by her daughter, Louise (Little Baby). Photo courtesy of John N. Smith Restoration and Preservation, Inc.

Figure 7 In 1922 Karen Mosteller purchased a commemorative brick from the Southport Historical Society in honor of Annie. It sits in front of Fort Johnston Southport Museum and Visitors' Center. Photo credit: Lawrence N. Ashley.

What happened to Annie's daughter?

Annie's Daughter, Maggie Louise Clemmons, grew up being called "Little Baby", but as an adult, she preferred to be called Louise. Although Louise never knew her father, she was surrounded by love from her family, her friends, and her church community.

Louise always loved books. She read everything she could get her hands on. She would have given anything to be able to go to the public library in Southport and read the books there, but until the mid-1960s, the library was for Whites only.

When the Brunswick County Training school was built in 1920, it's likely Louise was excited. The idea of going to school in a brand new, clean building that contained four individual classrooms, with large windows and whitewashed walls, must have been thrilling. But then before Louise or any of the students were able to attend a single class, the school burned down to the ground. So, in the end, instead of going to a brand-new school, Louise went to the old, drafty building where the children all crowded into a single classroom.

After the initial shock of the fire wore off, Louise's mother and the other Brunswick County Black parents set about raising money all over again. When they had enough, they applied for another grant from the Rosenwald Foundation.[93]

Founded in 1917 by Julius Rosenwald and his family, the Rosenwald Fund, also known as the Julius Rosenwald Foundation, was a philanthropic institution. During the 1910s to the 1930s, its principal focus centered on education in North Carolina. Through matching grants, the fund facilitated the construction of over eight hundred public school buildings, all of them intended specifically for North Carolina's Black children.

Brunswick County Training School #2 turned out to be even bigger than the first school they had built. This school had six or seven separate classrooms. But by the time it was completed, Louise was twelve years old. It had been a long time to wait. Still, she was glad she was able to finish her schooling and not have to stop at the 8th grade.

Louise loved her mama and her family and her little corner of Southport. But she must have felt like there wasn't enough opportunity for her in Southport. She had so much to offer, but there was no place to give it in her hometown.

So, when Walter Dooley came along and told her he could show her the world, she agreed to go. She might have hoped that she would someday return to Southport to settle down, but in their hearts, she and her mother both knew that would never happen.

Walter, born and raised in Tennessee, had enlisted in the military at the beginning of WWII. He was an educated man who already had three years of college. Before the war, he worked as a chemist at Quaker City Chemicals in Morrell, Tennessee. After enlistment, Walter was stationed at Fort Bragg. At some point, he came to Southport where he and Louise met and fell in love.[94]

Walter decided to make a career out of the military, serving overseas in both WWII and the Korean conflict. After twenty-three years in the service, he retired from active duty. He then spent another twenty years in Fort Bliss Civil Service working as an Electronics Instructor.[95]

By all accounts, Louise enjoyed being a military wife. She became a librarian at Fort Bliss and in Beaumont, Texas, fulfilling her childhood dream of being able to read all the books she wanted.[96]

Louise and Walter never had any children. But she remained close to her Southport cousins and had several dear friends who constituted her family.

She and Walter built a beautiful home in Texas. They were both Catholic and were very active members of their church. Louise enjoyed collecting dolls and they both enjoyed the theater and going out to dinner. Louise continued to stay close to her mother, writing and visiting regularly. Louise was forty-three when her mother passed away. She came home to Southport for her funeral and had a special marker made that said "My Beloved Mother. Rest In Peace. Gone But Not Forgotten".

When she was seventy-nine her husband, Walter, passed away from cancer. With the help of a yardman and a housekeeper, Louise was able to continue to live independently in her own home, until she passed away at the age of ninety-four.[97]

Figure 8 Louise Clemmons Dooley and Walter A. Dooley. Photo courtesy of the Clemmons Family.

What happened to the rest of Annie Clemmons' family?

Annie had seven brothers and one sister who survived to adulthood. They all took different paths in life. But the values that Annie's parents, Allen and Martha Clemmons, had of education, service to the community, and the importance of the vote continue to be passed on from generation to generation. Here are a few of the accomplishments of the family.

Allen Clemmons (1879 – post 1940)

Annie's oldest brother Allen married Sarah Gray. They moved to Elizabethtown where he owned and operated a grocery store. He owned a home that was valued at $400 in 1940. Despite the challenges of obtaining an education in the 1880s, he achieved a 4th-grade education.[98]

Allen's son Dexter moved back to Southport and became a business owner. He owned HiWay Cleaners which was also known as the "Pressing Club". In a time when segregation was the norm, Dexter's business became popular in the entire Southport community.[99] He passed the business on to his son and daughter-in-law Lorenzo and

Marjorie Clemmons. In 1963 Dexter's daughter-in-law Marjorie and his other son, Allen, Jr. were two of the founders of the Southport NAACP which worked to eliminate segregation in Southport and advance voting and other civil rights.[100]

Charles Henry (1882 – post 1937)

Not much is known about Annie's brother, Charles. He worked as a cook on a U.S. Government boat in Southport and was married to a woman named Minnie.[101]

Katie (1885 – 1937)

In 1905, at the age of nineteen, Annie's only sister, Katie, married Joseph Green, a fisherman. The couple had four children, three of whom survived to adulthood. Her older daughter, Martha, named after her grandmother, became a public-school teacher. Her younger daughter, Jessie Inez, helped care for her Aunt Annie Clemmons in her declining years. The couple owned their own home on St. George Street, valued at $1200 in 1930.[102]

Israel (Ezra) Preston (1886 – 1939)

In 1911, Annie's brother, Israel, married Mary Merrick though they later divorced. His first job was working as a waiter on the dredge boat *Cape Fear*. He later ran a filling station in Southport.[103]

Joseph Anthony (1888 – 1940)

Annie's brother, Joseph, was part of the Great Migration of southern Blacks who moved north during the first part of the 20th century. As painful as it was to leave their families and friends, they left to escape the oppression of segregation, and the threat of racial violence, and to pursue economic and educational opportunities.

While several of Annie's brothers moved north for a while, Joseph is the only one to remain there. He moved to Newark, NJ where he worked as a laborer in a chemical company. He lived in a rental home with his wife Francis. Always ambitious, Joseph achieved the highest level of education that was available in Brunswick during his adolescence, graduating from the 8th grade.[104]

George Allen (1894 – 1967)

Annie's brother George achieved two years of high school education. He worked as a commercial fisherman and shrimper. In 1914, he married Rosa Hankins, who worked as a laundress. The couple owned their own home on Clarendon Avenue, valued at $300 in 1940. George is remembered as being an entertaining storyteller with a good sense of humor. His son, Edward, was a faculty member of Livingstone College. His great-grandson, James Edward Clemmons, Jr. became the first Black Sheriff of Richmond County, North Carolina.[105]

James Franklin (1896 – 1960)

Although all of Annie's brothers registered for the draft in WWI, only James Franklin was inducted. He served in Co. D. 349th, Labor Battalion. He later worked for the U.S. Government as a cook on a dredge boat. In 1920, he married Julia Frances Joyner. Miss Julia had a variety store in a two-story building next to her home which was located about half a block from Brunswick County Training School. Schoolchildren would stop by with their few pennies to buy small items they could afford such as pickles, chips, sodas, candies, homemade pies, and gum. The couple had four children.[106]

John Elmore (1900 – 1994)

The youngest of Annie's siblings, John worked as a fisherman for a Southport fish factory. In 1922, he married Elsie Joyner. They owned a house on Dry Street valued at $1000 in 1930. They had five children together.[107]

Frequently Asked Questions About NC Black Voting Rights

Elizabeth Stanford Fuller, PhD

How did NC Black men obtain the right to vote?

Following the Civil War, the issue of voting rights for Black men sparked controversy in both the North and the South. At that time, only a handful of Northern states allowed Black men to vote. Surprisingly, even some Northern abolitionists, who had ardently advocated for the freedom of enslaved individuals, did not fully support granting freedmen the right to vote.

The passion against Black voting rights was particularly strong in the South due in part to the sizable population of four million freedmen. North Carolina, where a third of the population had been enslaved, was no exception. The concern was greatest in eastern counties, like Brunswick and New Hanover, where the population of Black citizens outnumbered the Whites.

Throughout the South, this situation fueled a prevailing fear that allowing Black men to vote would tip the scales in elections, potentially leading to the subjugation of the White citizenry. The irony was that in the absence of voting rights, Black people were the ones who were being subjugated.

Southern governments, led by many of the same men who had governed the Confederacy, quickly replaced antebellum Slave codes with similarly worded Black codes that severely restricted the rights of the formerly enslaved.

North Carolina's Black code pertained to anyone who had at least one Black great-grandparent. With no voting rights, they had no means of overturning these laws.[108]

Black North Carolinians were not permitted to vote, serve on juries, or testify against Whites in court. They could not marry anyone who was not Black. They could not enter into a contract with another Black person unless they created a written document and had it witnessed by a White person.

It was illegal for Black people to be unemployed. Anyone found guilty of vagrancy could be assigned to work crews and be hired out as unpaid labor to private railways, mines, and large plantations, thus creating a legalized version of slavery.

Once employed, Black workers had a difficult time leaving for other opportunities, regardless of their work conditions. The Black Code included an "anti-enticement law" that prohibited any potential employer from enticing an employee away from an existing job.

Black parents had limited say over their children's lives. Former enslavers had the right to take the children of those they had enslaved without parental permission. By appointing themselves guardians, they could put the children into unpaid apprenticeships, thus obtaining free labor.

The code also defined new standards for criminal behavior. The mere "intent" to steal was considered a crime. And the penalty for a Black man who "attempted" to rape a White woman was death.

As far as President Andrew Johnson was concerned, such laws were the business of the states. His only stipulations for reconstruction were that the states declare secession null and void, abolish slavery, and repudiate their war debt. Former Confederate citizens, including members of the military, could restore their citizenship and regain their property by swearing a loyalty oath. Officers and government leaders had to apply directly to Johnson for a pardon, which he freely granted.

In accordance with the Presidential plan, North Carolina's Governor called for a special convention that set out to meet the minimum requirements for re-entry into the Union. The convention which met in

October 1865, approved ordinances that abolished slavery, declared the previous secession amendment null and void, and repudiated all war time debts. Then, for the first time since 1860, North Carolina and several other Southern states sent representatives to serve in the next session of Congress.

However, when the 39th Congress assembled in December 1865, members refused to admit the Southern representatives, some of whom had served in the Confederate government. Congress was within its rights to do so as the U.S. Constitution gives Congress, not the President, the right to be the judge of the elections, returns, and qualifications of its own members.[109]

Military Reconstruction

Congress then reviewed Johnson's Presidential Reconstruction Plan and determined it to be inadequate. Because the plan failed to require substantial changes by the South, the majority of members believed it undermined the Northern victory and invalidated the nation's four-year sacrifice.

Instead, Congress drafted its own plans for reconstruction. Johnson vetoed the Acts every step of the way, but Congress overrode his vetoes to pass the Civil Rights Act of 1866, and the Military Reconstruction Plan.

This plan divided the former Confederate states into territories occupied by the military. In order to restore Congressional representation, each state was required to create and approve a new constitution that abolished slavery and established universal male suffrage. The states were also required to ratify the 13th Amendment which abolished slavery, and the 14th Amendment which established birthright citizenship.

To draft the new constitutions, each state was required to conduct a constitutional convention. Black men were eligible to serve as delegates to the convention and to participate in the election process by voting. Individuals who had held positions as officers in the Confederacy or had served in the Confederate government were not permitted to serve as delegates to the convention.

In 1867, the U.S. military oversaw the registration of Black men across the South. In North Carolina, seventy-thousand voters were added to the electorate, raising the number of registered voters to one-hundred-eighty thousand.

North Carolina's military governor then called for an election to select men to serve as delegates to a constitutional convention. Black men lined up alongside White men at the polls. As they cast their first-ever votes, federal soldiers stood guard to prevent interference and violence.

Allen Clemmons was only thirteen years old when that first election took place. Did he understand the significance of the day? When he witnessed the Black men in Lockwood's Folly heading to the polls, did he imagine himself doing the same someday when he became a man?

Abraham Galloway

Thirteen of the 120 convention delegates were Black men, elected to represent nineteen counties with Black majorities. One of the New Hanover delegates was Abraham Galloway who had been born on a Smithville Township plantation.[110] He was the son of Hester Hankins, an enslaved woman, and John Wesley Galloway, a Cape Fear River pilot,

Both father and son served in the Civil War, although they had supported opposing sides. The elder Galloway led the Coast Guard, North Carolina Volunteers, known as Capt. John W. Galloway's Company. Conversely, his son, who had escaped from slavery at the age of nineteen and journeyed north to collaborate with abolitionists, worked in support of the Union.

Early in the war, Abraham Galloway returned to North Carolina at great personal risk. He worked as a spy for the Union and recruited hundreds of men for the United States Colored Troops. He also took part in a five-man delegation of Black men who traveled to the nation's capital. There, they met with Abraham Lincoln to discuss postwar plans for Black civil rights.

After the war, Abraham Galloway shifted his focus to state politics. A compelling speaker, he ardently advocated for the rights of freed individuals. Serving as a delegate in North Carolina's Constitutional Convention, he assumed a prominent leadership position and passionately voiced his viewpoints.

The resulting Constitution of 1868 was the most democratic in the state's history, which had historically been run by an oligarchy of wealthy eastern planters. The convention delegates were required to abolish slavery and establish universal male suffrage. However, they went beyond this directive to reduce the centralized power of the General Assembly.

They gave more power to the people by having state and county officials elected by popular vote. They eliminated racial and property requirements for holding public office. They restructured the criteria for determining state senate representation so that it was based on population rather than wealth.

They overhauled the judicial system, creating another level of judges who were elected by their constituents. They eliminated whipping as a punishment and reduced the number of crimes that were punishable by death. They called for tuition-free public education for all students between the ages of six and twenty-one regardless of race.

The proposed constitution stirred profound controversy among the public. Conservatives were alarmed by the reduction in power for wealthy landowners and the accompanying rise in power for Black and poor White voters. Additionally, the omission of any reference to segregation in public schools troubled many, raising fears of possible amalgamation, or the blending of the races.

Despite the controversy, the Constitution of 1868 was adopted by a vote of 93,086 to 74,016. New Hanover voted in favor of the constitution 3,571 to 2,235. However, in Brunswick County, the proposed constitution failed by a single vote, 784 to 785.[111]

North Carolina Conservatives suffered another blow when the Republican party emerged victorious in the 1868 elections. Voter turnout more than doubled compared to 1866, with most of the new voters supporting the Republican party.[112]

With North Carolina now having been readmitted to the Union, the impact was felt at the national level and state level. Both U.S. Senators and six of the seven newly elected Congressmen were Republican. The state's nine electoral votes went for Grant, with Abraham Galloway becoming North Carolina's first Black state elector.

William W. Holden became North Carolina's first Republican governor, and the General Assembly held a sizeable Republican majority. In Brunswick and New Hanover, Abraham Galloway was elected one of the two state senators representing their combined district. In total three Black state senators and seventeen state representatives were elected to North Carolina's General Assembly of 1868.

Galloway took as strong a leadership role in the state senate as he had in the Constitutional Convention. He consistently fought for the rights of Black citizens, as well as representing the concerns of all his constituents. In his words, he came here to help the poor White man, as well as the colored man, and to do justice to all men.[113]

Galloway wanted justice for women as well. Fifty years before Annie Clemmons ever tried to register to vote, Abraham Galloway was working for women's suffrage. In 1869 and 1870, he introduced bills to amend North Carolina's constitution to give women the right to vote.[114]

How did the NC Ku Klux Klan try to stop Black voters?

The rapid transformation that allowed Black men to progress from slavery to suffrage within three years caused considerable resentment among White citizens in North Carolina. Witnessing Black men and women freely moving about, working, and sending their children to school served as a constant reminder of the recent defeat and the drastic economic decline experienced by the White community.

Some White citizens refused to accept the legitimacy of the postwar government that had been established under military occupation. They disagreed with the laws that protected the rights of Black citizens and felt the law was not doing enough to protect them.

They expressed their anger in acts of violence toward Black citizens and toward the White Republicans who were encouraging them to vote. In 1867, Reverand A.G. Smith of Smithville's Methodist Episcopal Church for the Colored reported some of these incidents to the Freedmen's Bureau. He reported an incident in which a Black man was shot at for no reason and stated that the entire county was in a very unsettled state.[115]

In 1868, this bitter resentment found an outlet when the Ku Klux Klan arrived in Orange County, North Carolina. From there it swiftly expanded across the Piedmont region. What were once isolated acts of violence turned into coordinated terrorist attacks as more men joined the ranks.

Donning masks and robes to conceal their identities and to strike fear in those who saw them, White men rode through the night across the countryside. They forcibly pulled families from their homes, whipping, lynching, shooting, burning, raping, and assaulting their victims. They stole guns and other belongings and set homes, barns, and schools ablaze.

During a single ten-month period in 1869-70, Piedmont Klan members committed twelve murders, nine rapes, eleven arsons, and seven mutilations. Four or five thousand houses were broken open and their possessions stolen. Seven or eight hundred people were beaten or mistreated.[116]

Ku Klux Klan in Wilmington and Smithville

It would be a mistake to think that Klan activity only occurred in the Piedmont region. Although this was the worst area, it was also prevalent in Jones, Lenoir, and Rutherford Counties, all areas where the White population outnumbered the Blacks. Although there were some reported instances in New Hanover and Brunswick, the Klan had a more difficult time gaining a foothold in these majority Black counties.

In 1868, the Ku Klux Klan came to Wilmington under the direction of Col. Roger Moore. Thirty-year-old Moore was a former Confederate officer, a regimental officer of the New Hanover County militia, and a descendant of "King" Roger Moore who had been the founder of Orton plantation, the largest in Brunswick County. He journeyed to Raleigh to be installed as "Chief of the Division of the Ku Klux Klan in Wilmington."[117]

Then, beginning just a few weeks before the 1868 election, local newspapers attempted to frighten Black citizens by reporting the sightings of a skeletal ghost of a Confederate soldier roaming Wilmington's streets.

The ghost's ominous message was said to be:

"The Ku Klux are abroad! The Avenger cometh with the night when man sleepeth! Beware! The hour is near at hand!"[118]

After a few days of these types of articles, the newspaper printed a very different article indicating that Black citizens had begun retaliating against this type of intimidation and threats. Rather than waiting to be attacked in their homes, a dozen Black Wilmington men patrolled the streets of their neighborhoods to discourage attacks. Arming themselves with guns and fence rails, they challenged any White men they encountered.[119]

In this instance, the Black citizens of Wilmington were successful in discouraging Klan attacks. Col. Roger Moore soon distanced himself from a formal Klan organization, nighttime incidents faded away and Wilmington remained peaceful - at least for the time being.

Klan activities in Brunswick County from that period are not well documented. However, there are indications that the Klan was there. As late as 1876, Lewis Galloway, the White secretary of the Brunswick County Republican party reported, "the entire meeting seemed to be of one opinion, that all they had to do was to give one hearty pull, and all pull together, and old Brunswick would be redeemed from her K.K. [Ku Klux] rule and extravagance."[120]

Klan Terrorism Escalates

The Klan targeted both Black and White Republicans and their families. The masked perpetrators were seldom held accountable for their crimes. Klan members routinely swore false alibis for one another. In many towns, Klan membership included business and government leaders and police officers. As a result, arrests were seldom made.

On the few occasions Klan members were brought to trial, local juries would not convict. Some jurors were themselves members of the Klan, while others were sympathetic to the Klan's actions.

Jurors who disapproved of Klan actions refused to find them guilty out of fear of reprisal to themselves or their families. Frustrated judges such as Sam Watts and Albert Tourgee complained to the governor that they could not get juries to convict even in the face of overwhelming evidence.[121]

With no legal consequences for their actions, Klan violence grew more and more brazen. On February 26, 1870, a mob of sixty masked men stormed the home of Constable Wyatt Outlaw, a veteran of the US Colored Troops, and the first Black man to serve as Constable and Town Commissioner in Graham, North Carolina. Torn from the arms of his family, Outlaw was abducted, tortured, and lynched from a tree that stood within 20 yards of the Alamance County courthouse.[122]

Three months later, John Stephens, a White Republican State Senator in Caswell County, was murdered inside the Yanceyville courthouse. For quite some time, Stephens had been working to encourage Black men to vote for the Republican Party. This had infuriated many of his White neighbors who considered him a scalawag, or a traitor to his Southern brethren.

On this particular night, Frank Wiley, a former County Sheriff and a man whom Stephens believed to be his friend, tricked Stephens into entering the lowest floor of the courthouse. There, several waiting men jumped him, stabbing him repeatedly before strangling him with a rope. They then hid his body in a locked room where it was discovered the next day.

Insurrection

Governor William Holden was shocked by the violence occurring in his state and the apparent inability of local authorities to control it. With the use of detectives and undercover agents, he determined that in some cases police officers, business leaders, and government officials were members of the secret terrorist organizations.[123] Where they were not active participants, they were often too frightened of reprisal to take action.

At a loss, Holden appealed to the Republican-controlled General Assembly. State Senator T.M. Shoffner introduced a bill that would empower the governor to suspend habeas corpus and to use a militia to restore order in the counties that were being overrun by terrorists.

Shoffner, who represented Alamance County, stated that his own constituents had implored him to do something to protect them. He said he was submitting the bill despite having received death threats for doing so.

Several senators objected to the proposal stating that the counties had sufficient means to put down the violence without invoking martial law. They even intimated that in some cases the Klan's actions were a necessary evil.

Sen. Abraham Galloway countered their argument by stating,

> "There is a disposition on the part of gentlemen of a certain political party to justify the deeds and outrages of this miserable and contemptible organization [Ku Klux Klan]. When I reflect in my mind I can but come to one conclusion in this matter: that it is the purpose and understanding of the Democratic party to oppose everything for the benefit of society and give more power to these miserable murderers who are now troubling the entire country. I will ask senators here if it is law or the enforcement of law when every other day a murder is committed."[124]

Shoffner's bill was approved the following month, in January 1870. Abraham Galloway and Edwin Legg, the two senators representing Brunswick and New Hanover Counties voted in favor of the bill which read.

> " The governor is hereby authorized whenever in his judgment the civil authorities in any county are unable to protect its citizens in the enjoyment of life and property, to declare such county to be in a state of insurrection and to call into active service the militia of

the state to such an extent as may become necessary to suppress such insurrection; and in such case the governor is further authorized to call upon the president for such assistance if any, as, in his judgment, may be necessary to enforce the law."[125]

Two months later, in April 1870, Holden declared Alamance to be in a state of insurrection and put the county under martial law. He did the same for Caswell County in May. He then sent a militia of three hundred men under the direction of Col. George W. Kirk to subdue the violence. Kirk's men arrested over one hundred suspected Klansmen without serious incident. Those arrested included both the Caswell and Alamance County sheriffs and former U.S. Congressman John Kerr, Jr.[126]

The prisoners were detained in Caswell County until they could be tried by a special military court. A state judge issued writs of habeas corpus, but these legal orders were ignored by Kirk and Holden. At that point, the imprisoned vigilantes, who had demonstrated no concern for their victims' rights to life, property, and due process, appealed to the federal courts to have their own civil rights enforced.

Upon reviewing the situation, President Grant informed Holden that the federal government could not support the actions the governor had taken to protect North Carolina's citizens from terrorist attacks. Consequently, the prisoners were released.

The Democratic press condemned the governor's actions, derisively calling it the "The Kirk-Holden War." The public turned against Holden and the burgeoning Republican Party.

In multiple North Carolina towns, State Senator T. M. Shoffner's likeness was burned in effigy. He received so many death threats that the adjutant General of the state offered to furnish federal troops for his protection. That spring, at the end of his senate term, Shoffner packed up his family and fled the county of his birth, never to return. Instead, he relocated to Indiana and built a new life there.[127]

Just a few months later, in November 1870, a statewide election was held. Intimidated by the unchecked terrorist attacks, many Republicans stayed home from the polls. Consequently, the Democrats swept the election, retaking control of the General Assembly (111 Dem to 53 Rep).

Governor Impeached, Klan Given Amnesty

The new conservative state legislature immediately set to work. Their first order of business was to impeach Governor Holden for overstepping his authority. His trial, begun at the end of January 1871, lasted seven weeks. After which, he was convicted, becoming the first U.S. governor to be removed from office.

Two years later, in 1873, the General Assembly issued a general amnesty bill pardoning any member of a secret society such as the Ku Klux Klan who had committed any crime (excluding murder, rape, arson, or burglary) prior to September 1, 1871. The following year, they expanded the amnesty to pardon those who had committed arson, burglary, or murder.[128]

Legacy of Senator Abraham Galloway

No one will ever know what Abraham Galloway thought of Governor Holden being impeached or of his senate colleague Shoffner being run out of the state. Galloway's strident voice had been forever silenced in September 1870.

As was demonstrated in his earlier arguments with fellow senators over the outrages perpetrated by the Klan, Galloway could be confrontational when pursuing a cause he deeply believed in. He stood his ground, even when arguing with White opponents. This bold and fearless behavior flew in the face of all social expectations that demanded Black men behave subserviently.

Galloway was aware of the risks his behavior courted. He knew his demeanor drew a large target on his back. More than once he had been the near victim of an assassin's knife or an angry mob's noose.

Most men in his position would have chosen to soften their approach. But Galloway was never like most men. In a time when Black men were not even supposed to own a gun, Galloway chose to wear a pistol in his belt, boldly displaying it, for all to see.

It's possible that Galloway never expected to live a long life. Since adolescence, he had taken risk after risk to advance his goals. Despite the rapid post-war gains that had been made by Black men in his home state, he always seemed impatient for more. So, it might not have come as a surprise to him, when his life was cut short, ending abruptly at the age of thirty-three.

Rather than the assassin's bullet that he had almost seemed to invite, Galloway was struck down by common illness on the eve of his second term in the Senate. He had struggled with chronic health problems for a while, but when the end came, it was sudden. His wife and two small children were out of town, but his mother was by his side.

One newspaper estimated that Abraham Galloway's funeral was attended by upwards of six thousand mourners, including multiple Black organizations such as the Masonic Lodge and several Black fire departments. More than a hundred vehicles, including a delegation from the state's General Assembly, formed the funeral procession that led from his mother's home to St. Paul's Episcopal Church for the service.[129]

Black men and women from New Hanover and nearby counties made their way to the funeral. It's likely men from Smithville Township, possibly even sixteen-year-old Allen Clemmons, journeyed up the Cape Fear River to bid their final farewells to the man whose life had started out so like their own, and to make a pledge to never give up on the work that he had so masterfully begun.

Elizabeth Stanford Fuller, PhD

How did NC's government try to stop Black men from voting?

Despite their 1870 victory, the Democrats (as the Conservative Party was starting to refer to itself) were concerned about the potential for future Republican impact on state and national elections. They began to consider ways they could limit future Republican influence in the state.

The first opportunity that presented itself was the map that defined the congressional districts. Like most Southern states, North Carolina gained an extra Congressional seat following the 1870 census. This is because the freedpeople were now being fully counted rather than the previous approach that only counted three-fifths of the enslaved population.

As the General Assembly redrew the maps, they looked for a way to squeeze most of the counties with a Black majority into one district. They knew that this district would vote Republican, but they hoped that the rest of the districts would vote Democrat. They were willing to sacrifice one congressional seat out of eight.

The result was the very oddly shaped, gerrymandered second district, which became known as "the Black Second,". This district included Craven, Jones, Halifax, Northampton, Warren, Edgecombe, Greene, Lenoir, Wayne, and Wilson counties. It did not include Brunswick and New Hanover Counties, with 42% and 58% Black populations respectively. These counties became part of the Third Congressional District.[130]

Figure 9 Congressional District maps based on the 1870 U.S. census. District Two contains most of the counties with a Black majority.

The redistricting plan worked precisely as the state legislature had envisioned. North Carolina's first four Black U.S. Congressmen were all from the Black Second District.

In order, they were:
- John Hyman (1875 – 1877), a former North Carolina state legislator
- James O'Hara (1883 – 1887), a Howard University graduate and the third Black lawyer admitted to the North Carolina Bar
- Henry P. Cheatham (1889 – 1893), a master's degree graduate from Shaw University
- George H. White (1897-1901), a graduate of Howard University and a licensed North Carolina attorney.

Figure 10 Top Row John Hyman, James O'Hara Bottom Row Henry P. Cheatham, George Henry White congressmen from District Two. Photos Library of Congress.

Over the course of twenty-six years, these men provided a voice for a segment of North Carolina's population that had never been represented in the nation's government. During their terms, they submitted multiple bills on issues that were important to their constituents.

Some examples are bills to: [131]
- reimburse depositors of the failed Freedmen's Bank (Cheatham, O'Hara)
- honor Robert Smalls and the crew of the *Planter* for their service during the Civil War (Cheatham)
- add a civil rights amendment to the U.S. Constitution (O'Hara)
- prevent segregation of railroad passengers (O'Hara)
- investigate the 1886 attack on a Carrolton, MS courthouse, which resulted in the death of twenty-three Black men (O'Hara)

115

- increase public education in the South (White)
- require equal pay for male and female teachers (O'Hara)
- reduce the representation of states that prevent Black citizens from voting (White)
- make lynching a federal crime punishable by death (White)

Despite their best efforts, none of these bills passed. Hyman, the first Black Congressman from North Carolina also submitted bills, but none made it out of committee.

The Clemmons family would have been aware of these Congressmen who were from the eastern part of North Carolina. But because they lived in Brunswick County, which was part of District Three, Allen Clemmons would never have had a chance to vote for any of them.

Congressman George Henry White left office at the end of his term in March 1901. He did not run again as he knew that North Carolina's new voter suppression tactics would prevent him from winning.

On that last day of his term, as the final Black United States Congressman took leave of his post, the White legislators in Raleigh celebrated.

North Carolina State legislator, A. D. Watts announced:

> "George H. White, the insolent negro...has retired from office forever. And from this hour on no negro will again disgrace the old State in the council of chambers of the nation. For these mercies, thank God."[132]

While it wouldn't be forever, it would be more than ninety years before another Black North Carolina Representative was sent to the United States Congress.

Changes to Voting Laws

The conservative party remained in control of the General Assembly through several subsequent elections. The much smaller, predominantly Black Republican Party posed no real threat to their dominance. Still, the General Assembly continued to look for ways to suppress Black suffrage.

In 1875, the legislature called a constitutional convention to amend the controversial Constitution of 1868. A main priority for the constitutional delegates was to restrict voter participation.

They made an amendment extending the voter residency requirement from thirty days to ninety days.[133] On the surface, this appears to be a race-neutral policy. But because Black workers often needed to follow seasonal jobs, Black families tended to be more transient than their White counterparts. As a result, the residency requirement disproportionately affected the eligibility of Black North Carolinians.

A second amendment permanently disenfranchised anyone convicted of a felony.[134] Since Black men were more likely to be arrested, charged, and convicted of crimes, this law disproportionately impacted their ability to vote. Both amendments were ratified by the public in 1875.

What happened to NC Black voters when Reconstruction ended?

Reconstruction came to an abrupt end in 1877 following the election of President Rutherford B. Hayes. Many in the North had begun to feel they had done enough for the freedpeople and that it was time for them to stand on their own two feet. Since 1873, the U.S. had been experiencing a severe economic downturn, known as the Long Depression. Policing the South had become an expense that the nation was no longer interested in supporting.

When military occupation ended across the South, the reconstructed states were given full autonomy to run their own affairs. Almost immediately, across the South, Black men had their right to vote taken away through voter suppression, intimidation, and violence.

For two decades, North Carolina stood out as an exception. Black voter engagement remained notably high throughout the latter part of the 19th century. Since the Democratic Party had firm control of the legislature, they didn't feel the need to take drastic measures to suppress Black voter participation, as many Southern states did. Despite their best efforts, Republican voting had almost no effect on the outcome of state and national elections.

From 1877 to 1897, Democrats held sway over the state legislature, controlling both the General Assembly and the governorship. During that span, all U.S. Senators representing North Carolina were Democrats, along with an average of 80% of the state's Congressional representatives. Additionally, North Carolina backed all Democratic Presidents during this period.

A New Threat to Democratic One-Party Rule

In 1892, the new Populist Party formed its first chapter in North Carolina. This party appealed to rural White farmers who felt their concerns for public schools, better roads, and decentralized government were being overlooked. Members of the Democratic Party began to peel off and join the Populists also known as the People's Party.

The impact of this emerging party on Southport's election of 1892 remains uncertain. Several Populist candidates were on the ballot, including I.W. Harrelson who was running for state senate. However, the true outcome of the race remains unknown because all of the Populist and Republican ballots were discarded, leaving only the Democrat ballots to be tallied.

After the polls closed, the Board of Canvassers assembled at Southport's County Courthouse to conduct the ballot count. As they progressed, they reached the vote for the state senate. It was then noted by canvasser E.L. Stanley of Lockwood's Folly that the Republican and Populist ballots were printed on cream-colored paper, not the required white paper.

Stanley made a motion that the Republican ballots be discarded. This motion passed with seven canvassers approving and only canvassers R.M. Wescott and Spencer from Southport dissenting.

Subsequently, Stanley made a second motion that the third-party Populist ballots be discarded for the same reason. This motion was also approved. Once again seven canvassers were in favor. Only R.M. Wescott opposed the motion, while John M. Tharp of Town Creek abstained.

Wescott who was a merchant from Southport, defended his dissent, saying "he did not consider the ballots sufficiently colored to warrant their being thrown out."[135]

The only non-Democrat candidate to win in that County-wide election was John Evans, a Black candidate running unopposed for Constable of Smithville Township who received 156 votes.[136] Following the election, four hundred men met at the courthouse in Southport to voice their objections to the way the election was handled. In addition to the discard of votes, there was also testimony about voter suppression at the polls. There were several accounts of men being challenged at the polls and prevented from voting. Despite these protests, the election count stood.[137]

The First U.S. Interracial Political Alliance

Even in a fair election in which all votes were counted, neither the predominantly Black Republican Party nor the all-White Populist Party posed a significant threat to the much larger and better established, conservative Democrat Party. But at some point, the leaders of the two smaller parties realized that if they "fused" together, the resulting alliance would shift the balance of power in their favor. If they agreed to support each other's candidates, they could achieve more together than they could separately.

The resulting Fusionist strategy proved to be very successful. The election of 1894 was the first time the two parties, Populist and Republican, worked together to run a combined ticket. The parties gained control of the North Carolina Supreme Court, the General Assembly, and most of the state's seats in Congress. They also sent two members to the U.S. Senate.

Fusionists Expand Voting Rights

The new Fusionist-controlled General Assembly made overhauling the state's election process a priority. They implemented a 25-page law called "An act to revise, amend and consolidate the election laws of North Carolina."[138]

Rather than being a partisan attempt to give themselves an advantage in the polls as the conservative Democrats had done, the act seems to have been a sincere effort to put order and structure around the state's election process. It spelled out consequences for voter fraud, intimidation, and coercion. Noted historian J. Morgan Kousser considers North Carolina's 1895 Suffrage Act "some of the fairest and most democratic election laws in the post-Reconstruction South." [139]

The Act also contained changes to the voting rules that made it easier for Black and rural White voters to participate. It created a system to limit unfair practices by having multiple registrars and electoral judges from the different parties present to oversee registration and voting. It changed the registration criteria so that prospective voters would be allowed to register even if they did not know their exact age or address, a common circumstance for older Black and rural White voters.

To reduce voter intimidation, the act made it harder to challenge prospective voters. Previously anyone standing at the election polls could challenge the eligibility of a voter to participate. Under the new law, if a voter's name was in the registration book, election officials were to assume the voter was properly registered. The new law also made it easier for illiterate voters to participate by allowing ballots to include symbols or to be printed on colored paper.

The new pro-Suffrage Act made a marked difference in voter participation. Republican registration rose among both Black and White voters. In the 1892 gubernatorial election, held prior to the 1895 Suffrage Act, Black voter participation was 62 percent. Four years later, Black voter participation was 87 percent, a level that hasn't been seen since in North Carolina.[140]

This progress did not come without some struggle. For some time, Black Brunswick County Republicans had been feeling underutilized. After thirty years in politics, they were still not receiving many nominations as candidates. The alliance with the Populist Party seemed to aggravate the situation.

Out of the 850 Republicans in Brunswick County, 750 were Black.[141] The all-White Populist Party was willing to team up with the Republican Party in order to gain votes, but they showed no interest in supporting a Black candidate. Despite this, most North Carolina Republicans maintained faith that this first-of-its-kind interracial alignment would pay off.

In fact, in 1896 a committee of members of the Republican party published an open letter in the Southport Leader newspaper reassuring the Republicans and Populist Parties that despite rumors to the contrary, the alliance still stood firm. Among those signing the letter were men who had been actively involved in Southport's politics and leadership for many years: Frank Gordon (educator), Frank Davis (Smithville's first Black postmaster), Judge Sam Watts (who worked against the KKK), Whitfield Griffin (church and community leader), Henry Hankins and Ben Fullwood (significant property owners).

The interracial alliance continued to hold together and in 1896 Daniel Russell, Jr. a White Republican from Brunswick County was elected Governor. The year after that, Wilmington held a hotly contested local election. When the dust finally settled, the city's newly elected mayor was a Fusionist, the majority of the aldermen were Radical Republicans, and three out of the ten aldermen were Black.[142]

What was the Wilmington Massacre of 1898?

By 1898, the conservative Democrat party in North Carolina was in full-blown panic. The fusion between the Republican and Populist parties had caused them to lose the previous three elections at the national, state, and local levels.

Furnifold Simmons, head of the North Carolina Democratic Party told the members that it was a mistake to try and win on the issues. Perhaps harkening back to the solidarity the party had experienced during Reconstruction, he suggested that they focus their message on race instead. They needed to remind the Populist party that they must stand with their White brethren. Anything else would lead to the dreaded "Negro rule."[143]

Simmons devised a three-fold plan based on "men who could speak, men who could write, and men who could ride."[144] Josephus Daniels, owner of the Raleigh News and Observer offered his newspaper as the voice of the Democratic party. He published sensationalized, racist articles and political cartoons that turned the public against the predominantly Black Republican party. He sold copies of his papers at cost to the Democrat party so they could be distributed to members for free.

Public speakers traveled around the state riling up the crowds with fiery white supremacist rhetoric. They described the threats to Southern

White womanhood posed by "burly, black, brutes" and the need to reassert dominance. In Wilmington, Alfred Moore Waddell gave a speech at Thalian Hall proclaiming they would overthrow "negro domination" even if "we have to choke the current of the Cape Fear with carcasses."[145]

Across the state, a White supremacist organization known as the Red Shirts began committing acts of terrorism against Black citizens. This group, which operated in broad daylight, was bolder and better organized than the Klan had been twenty years previously.

In Wilmington, groups of armed Red Shirts patrolled the city streets, loitering near Black churches and disrupting Black men wherever they gathered. The Wilmington Light Infantry went as far as procuring a Gatling gun, mounting it on a cart which they paraded around town and pointed at Black churches and other meeting places.

This relentless intimidation succeeded in its aim. On Election Day, many of Wilmington's Black voters chose to stay home and avoid trouble. To be extra sure of the outcome, ballot boxes in several precincts were stuffed with votes. In some instances, the number of ballots far outnumbered the number of registered voters.[146]

To no one's surprise, the conservative Democrat party carried the state. In Southport, Republican and Populist voters had been provided yellow ballots. When the votes were counted, these ballots were discarded by the canvassers due to not being printed on white paper.[147] In Southport, as in the rest of the state, Democrats won by a landslide.

While the majority of the state's Democrats celebrated a resounding victory, Wilmington's business leaders were planning the next phase of their strategy. This shadowy group of men wasn't willing to wait four months for the local election to remove the Fusionist mayor, sheriff, and city aldermen, a third of whom were Black.

Therefore, the day after the election, a gathering of exclusively White men convened at City Hall. During this meeting, they read aloud a document called the White Man's Declaration of Independence, in which they proclaimed their refusal to ever again submit themselves to what they termed "Negro rule."[148]

Afterward, the men called together several prominent Black business leaders and lawyers and read them the same Declaration of

Independence. They told them that they were charging them with closing down the town's Black newspaper or else the White men would destroy it themselves.

They gave the men until the next morning to respond. The concerned Black men composed a letter stating that the editor of the newspaper had already left town. The newspaper was already effectively shut down. They gave the letter to an attorney in the group but instead of hand delivering the letter, he left it in Waddell's mailbox where it went unnoticed.

The next morning hundreds of White men gathered at Thalian Hall. When they were informed that no letter had arrived, they angrily marched across town to the newspaper office of the Daily Record. There, they trashed the offices and destroyed the printing press, "accidentally" setting the building on fire in the process.

When they were finished, they marched back through the streets. At some point, they met up with Black men who had been at work when they heard their neighborhood was on fire. The unarmed men were hurrying home to check on their families.

No one knows how many men died that day. Current estimates are as many as sixty Black men were murdered.[149] Three White men suffered minor injuries. Frightened women and children ran into the swamps and hid, scared, alone, and shivering in the frigid November night. Some kept going, eventually reaching Southport, where they shared their stories of that horrible day and night.

Meanwhile, Waddell and a few other men made their way to the top floor of Thalian Hall. There they obtained the resignation at gunpoint of the mayor, the aldermen, and the sheriff. They marched the men through the streets, loaded them on a train, and told them to never come back. Waddell assumed the position of mayor and other insurrection leaders were sworn in as aldermen and sheriff.[150]

Pleas were made to Republican President McKinley. Congressman George H. White from North Carolina's Black Second district visited the White House personally requesting help for the people of Wilmington.[151] Black citizens who had endured the massacre wrote letters to Washington requesting help.

Twenty-two years before Anna Clemmons wrote her letters to the National Woman's Party, an anonymous Black woman from Wilmington, wrote her own letter to the President of the United States beseeching him for help.

Please send releif *[sic]* as soon as possible.
or we perish.

Wilmington N.C. Nov 13, 1898
Wm McKinley: -- President of the United States of America,

Hon- Sir,

I a Negro woman of this City appeal to you from the depths of my heart, to do something in the Negro's behalf. The outside world only knows one side of the trouble here, there is no paper to tell the truth about the Negro here, or in this or any other Southern state. The Negro in this town had no arms, (except pistols perhaps in some instances) with which to defend themselves from the attack of lawless whites. On the 10th Thursday morning between eight and nine o clock, when our Negro men had gone to their places of work, the white men led by Col. A. M. Waddell, Jno. D. Bellamy, & S. H. Fishblate marched from the Light Infantry armory on Market st. to Seventh down seventh to Love & Charity Hall (which was owned by a society of Negroes and where the Negro daily press was.) and set it afire & burnt it up And firing Guns Winchesters. They also had a Hotchkiss gun & two Colt rapid fire guns. We the negro expected nothing of the kind as they (the whites) had frightened them from the polls by saying they would be there with their shot guns. So the few that did vote did so quietly. And we thought after giving up to them and they carried the state it was settled. But they or Jno. D. Bellamy told them *[illegible words]* in addition to the guns they already had they could keep back federal interference. And he could have the Soldiers at Ft. Caswell to take up arms against the United States. After destroying the building they went over in Brooklyn another Negro settlement mostly, and began searching every one and if you did not submit, [you] would be shot down on the spot. They searched all the Negro Churches. And to day (Sunday) we dare not go to our places of worship. They found no guns or amunition *[sic]* in any of the places, for there was none. And to satisfy their Blood thirsty appetites would kill unoffending Negro men to or on their way from dinner. Some of our most worthy *[illegible]* Negro Men have been made to leave the City. Also some Whites, G. Z. French, Deputy Sheriff, Chief[sic] of police, Jno. R. Melton, Dr. S. P. Wright, Mayor, and R. H. Bunting, united states commissioner. We don't know where Mr. Chadbourn the Post Master is, and two or three others white. I call on you the head of the American Nation to help these humble subjects. We are loyal we go when duty calls us. And are we to die like rats in a trap? With no place to seek redress or to go with our Greiveances [sic]?

Can we call on any other Nation for help? Why do you forsake the Negro? Who is not to blame for being here. This Grand and Noble Nation who flies to the help of suffering humanity of another Nation? And leave the Secessionists and born Rioters to slay us. Oh, that we had never seen the light of the world. When our parents belonged to them, why, the Negro was all right. Now, when they work and accumalate [sic] property they are all wrong. The Negroes that have been banished are all property owners to considerable extent, had they been worthless negroes, we would not care.

Will you for God sake in your next message to Congress give us some releif [sic] If you send us all to Africa on we will be willing or a number of us will gladly go. Is this the land of the free and the home of the brave? How can the Negro Sing My Country tis of Thee? For Humanity's sake help us. For Christ sake do. We the Negro can do nothing but pray. There seems to be no help for us. No paper will tell the truth about the Negro. The Men of the 1st North Carolina were home on a furlough and they took a high hand in the nefarious work also. The Companies from every little town came in to kill the negro. There was not any Rioting Simply the strong slaying the weak. They speak of special police every white Man and boy from 12 years up had a gun or pistol, and the Negro had nothing, but his soul he could not say was his own. Oh, to see how we are Slaughtered, when our husbands go to work we do not look for their return. The Man who promises the Negro protection now as Mayor is the one who in his speech at the Opera house said the Cape Fear should be strewn with carcasses. Some papers I see, say it was right to eject the Negro editor That is all right but why should a whole city full of negroes suffer for Manly when he was hundred of miles away? And the paper had ceased publication. We were glad it was so for our own safety. But they tried to slay us all. To day we are mourners in a strange land with no protection near. God help us. Do something to alleviate our sorrows if you please. I cannot sign my name and live. But every word of this is true. The laws of our state is no good for the negro anyhow. Yours in much distress

Wilmington NC[152]

But Mayor Alfred Waddell told a different story than this woman described in her letter. He assured the federal government and the media that he and his men had successfully put down a race riot. He said they had reluctantly assumed control when the people of Wilmington had lost faith in the existing leadership. His message was that all was now well and there was nothing more to be done.[153] North Carolina's governor, Daniel Russel, backed up that story by refusing to ask for federal intervention.

And so, President McKinley, and Governor Daniel Russell, both of whom the Black Republicans of Wilmington had helped put into office just one year earlier, did nothing to help. They turned their backs on the people of Wilmington, allowing the only successful coup in the history of the United States to stand.

Congressman G.H. White, from North Carolina's Black Second District, made one last attempt to help the Black people of the South. He submitted a bill to Congress that would make murder by mob violence or lynching a federal crime. It failed to get out of committee.[154]

Following the election of 1898, the conservative Democratic Party dominated North Carolina politics for the next seventy years, only losing power after 1964, when the Party's platform changed to embrace civil and voting rights for all Americans.

How did NC's literacy test keep Black citizens from voting?

Within a few months of taking office, the Democratic General Assembly began seeking legal methods of suppressing Black voter participation. While the election of 1898 had been successful in its outcome, the methods used were not sustainable. There had been too much bloodshed, inviting too much public scrutiny. They needed a legal solution that would settle the matter once and for all.

Furnifold Simmons who had spearheaded the White Supremacist election campaign, now devised a plan to greatly reduce the Black voting population without running afoul of the 15th Amendment.

Working in conjunction with a politician named Charles Aycock who had been a prominent speaker during the White Supremacy campaign of 1898, he developed a plan to disenfranchise Black citizens without running afoul of the U.S. Constitution. He suggested a literacy test be required in order to register to vote. Since Black literacy in North Carolina at that time was approximately seventy percent, they could expect a thirty to forty percent reduction in Republican voters. It would be enough to help the conservative party stay in power.

Because literacy among White North Carolinians was comparably low, an exception, commonly referred to as the Grandfather Clause, was made for men who had a relative who had voted before January 1, 1867. Since the first time Black men participated in a North Carolina election was the statewide referendum of November 1867, this exception applied only to White men. Officially, this exception expired in 1908 at which time White applicants were also supposed to prove their literacy. But this was never enforced.

In 1900, Charles Aycock ran for governor, during the same election in which the so-called Suffrage Amendment was on the ballot. In his acceptance speech for the nomination, he stated.

> "Indeed it has become the fashion among Republicans and Populists to assert the unfitness of the negro to rule, but when they use the word rule, they confine it to holding office. When we say that the negro is unfit to rule we carry it one step further and convey the correct idea when we declare that he is unfit to vote. To do this we must disfranchise the negro. This movement comes from the people. Politicians have been afraid of it and have hesitated, but the great mass of white men in the State are now demanding and have demanded that the matter be settled once and for all. To do so is both desirable and necessary – desirable because it sets the white man free to move along faster than he can go when retarded by the slower movement of the negro."
> —*Charles Aycock, Address Accepting the Democratic Nomination for Governor, April 11, 1900*

The final version of the inaccurately named Suffrage Amendment, which also included a poll tax, passed, 182,217 to 128,285.[155] Newly elected Governor Charles Aycock oversaw its implementation in 1901.[156]

The amendment failed to pass in Brunswick County, by a margin of 143 votes. But in New Hanover, where the residents of Wilmington were still reeling from the aftermath of the massacre, it passed by a landslide. In the entire beleaguered city, only two voters dared to vote against the amendment.[157]

The legislature had anticipated a 30% drop in Black voter participation. Instead, there was a nearly 100% reduction. With this amendment, seventy-thousand Black voters were denied their constitutional right to vote.

The difference between the expectation and the outcome was due to the legislators underestimating the zeal with which the registrars would apply the tests. These local registrars had the discretion to pick any part of the Constitution for applicants to read and write, and they were granted the authority to assess literacy. Statewide, they categorized all Black voters, including professionals such as teachers and lawyers, as illiterate.

As Annie Clemmons discovered, the test was still being administered just as unfairly twenty years later when she attempted to register to vote.

If she could have been introduced to him, Annie would have sympathized with a young man named Henry Frye. Although Annie was forty-two when Henry was born, the two had much in common when it came to registering to vote.

Henry Frye was born in 1932 in Richmond County, North Carolina, the eighth child of tobacco and cotton farmers.[158] On August 21, 1956, just six months after Annie passed away, Henry was on his way to church to marry his sweetheart, Shirley, who had been waiting patiently for him while he served in the Air Force in Korea and Japan.

In those days there were only a few days that a person could register to vote, especially in rural areas. Frye's wedding day happened to fall on one of those days. So, before heading to the church, Captain Henry Frye decided to stop in at the registrar's office to register to vote. As an Honors graduate of AT&T College and an officer in the military, who had recently been accepted to law school, Henry didn't anticipate any problem with the literacy test.

However, instead of asking Henry to demonstrate his ability to read and write, the registrar pulled a book out of a drawer and began asking him to recite detailed sections of the 14th Amendment from memory, and to name the signers of the Declaration of Independence.

Henry challenged the registrar about the legality of his questions but was met with a dead-end. Just like Annie, there was no one he could raise a complaint to that day, especially if he was going to be on time for his wedding. So, Henry left the registrar's office and hurried off to marry Shirley.

As his bride walked down the aisle and met him at the altar, she could tell he was bursting to tell her something even before the ceremony began. Anticipating a few words about how lovely she looked, or how he couldn't wait to start their life together, she was surprised to hear him whisper, "Do you believe they wouldn't let me register to vote?"

Shirley asked that they discuss it later.

It must have been true love because Henry and Shirley remain married to this day. Just as Annie's rejection at the registrar had motivated her to write letters to the National Woman's Party, Henry's experience, which took place more than thirty years later, motivated him to take action as well.

In 1959 he graduated from the University of North Carolina School of Law where he had been the only Black student in his class. In 1963 he became an assistant U.S. Attorney, one of the first Black attorneys to hold that position in the South.

In 1968 he was elected to the North Carolina General Assembly as a state representative, the only Black legislator at that time. He was re-elected five more times, serving through 1980. He then served a term as a state senator while also teaching at North Carolina Central University's law school.

In 1983, Governor Jim Hunt appointed Frye to the North Carolina Supreme Court, the first Black jurist to hold that position in North Carolina's history. He was elected for two more eight-year terms before being appointed Chief Justice, the state's highest judicial post.[159]

There's little doubt that Judge Henry Frye is a man that Annie would have been happy to sit with on her porch and confide her secret to.

In 1919, North Carolina removed the poll tax as a requirement for voting, but the literacy test remained in force for over sixty years, until the Voting Rights Act of 1965 made it illegal. The test, especially the way it was implemented, had been an extremely successful tool for voter suppression. As late as 1948, only 15% of eligible Black voters were registered to vote in North Carolina. By 1968, three years after the passage of the Voting Rights Act, that percentage had reached 54%.

Although North Carolina's literacy test has been illegal since 1964, it is still part of the state constitution. During his time in the legislature, Frye tried to get the literacy test repealed and removed. His proposed repeal was approved by both chambers of the General Assembly but was subsequently voted down by the general public.

So, it remains in place, much like a Confederate statue positioned in front of a courthouse, serving as a reminder to all Black North Carolinians of the extent their fellow citizens were willing to go to prevent them from exercising their right to vote.[160]

Conclusion

Did Annie's letters help guarantee voting rights for Black citizens?

Of all the questions I get asked about Annie Clemmons, to me, this question about what she accomplished is the most important. Sometimes people are puzzled by the end of her story. They expect a tidy, happy ending in which Annie triumphantly marches to the polling booth, draws a curtain, pulls a lever, and casts her vote, a smile shining across her face.

But history is not a Hollywood movie, and events do not always occur in a prescribed timeline. The history of women's suffrage in the United States dates back to 1848 when the first women's rights convention was held in Seneca Falls, New York. Since then, history has been filled with women who devoted their entire lives to the issue of suffrage, only to die without ever being able to legally cast a vote: Lucretia Mott, Susan B. Anthony, Elizabeth Cady Stanton, Sojourner Truth, Frances Ellen Watkins Harper, to name a few.

To understand the significance of Annie's contribution, it's important to realize that in her lifetime, only a very small number of Black citizens participated in North Carolina elections.

As late as 1948 only 15% of eligible Black North Carolina voters were registered.[161] Due to intimidation, misinformation, and other interference tactics, a much smaller number went to the polls and voted.

It was not until 1965, nine years after Annie's death, that the federal Voting Rights Act (VRA) passed. This act, which passed without support from the Southern states, outlawed discriminatory voting practices like the literacy test that kept Annie from voting. It also gave the federal government authority to take over voter registration where patterns of persistent discrimination exist.

Within three years of the Voting Rights Act taking effect, Black voter registration in North Carolina surged to more than 50%.[162] It's important to recognize that even though Annie didn't live to witness the realization of her long-awaited "Enabling Act", her letters played a role in contributing to its eventual enactment. In the past 150 years, there have been many southern Black women who played a role in advancing voting rights. Some have names that are still remembered:

Mary Church Terrell – member of NAWSA, first president of the National Association of Colored Women (NACW), founder of the National Association of College Women, and a member of the National American Women Suffrage Association (NAWSA). BA (1884), MA (1888) from Oberlin University.

Mary Burnett Talbert – co-organized the Niagara Movement, a precursor to the National Association for the Advancement of Colored People (NAACP) and the beginning of 20th-century American civil rights activism. President (1916-1921) of the NACW. BA from Oberlin, class of 1886.

Septima Clark – created workshops on social justice and taught programs that combined literacy, rights, and duties of citizenship, and how to register to vote. BA from Benedict (1942) and MA from Hampton (1946).

Mary McLeod Bethune, Ph.D. – formed the National Council of Negro Women which initiated voter registration drives, lobbied for black appointments to strategic government positions, and promoted national legislation to abolish poll taxes and stop lynching. Honorary doctorates from eight colleges.

Ella Baker – helped organize the Southern Christian Leadership Conference (SCLC) and established the Student Nonviolent Coordinating Committee (SNCC). B.A. Shaw (1927)

Dorothy Cotton – director of the SCLC's Citizenship Education Program modeled on the work of Septima Clark. B.A. Va. State (1955) and M.A. Boston Univ. (1960)

Fannie Lou Hamer – testified to the Democratic National Committee about the horrors of violent voter suppression. Co-founded the National Women's Political Caucus. Hon. degrees from Columbia College Chicago (1970) and Howard (1972).

In addition, untold numbers of Black women contributed without recognition by praying, marching, organizing, fundraising, and of course, writing letters. The identities of most of these women will never be known. It's likely that many, like Annie, concealed their efforts due to fear of reprisal, or a belief that their individual contribution was too small to make a difference.

A hundred years after Annie penned her letters, her name and her contributions are no longer secret. The unveiling of her secret has provided substantial insights into the life of a solitary Black woman coming of age in early 20th-century Southport. However, Annie's legacy doesn't end there.

Her letters and her story also shine a light on the resilience of countless women who, against tremendous odds, did whatever they could, with whatever they had, to compel their country, the United States of America, to live up to its promise of democracy.

Every voice will be heard.

Every vote will be counted.

Acknowledgments

When you move to Southport, it's common to hear people say, *"I wasn't born in Southport, but I got here as soon as I could."* In my case, it took me fifty-six years of traveling on a long and circuitous route to find my way here, and I'm sure glad that I did.

Southport nurtures an exceptional community of individuals deeply invested in history, research, creativity, and connections, many of whom hang out at the Southport Historical Society. Somehow, I found my niche within this society, starting as a volunteer, advancing to Vice President, and eventually assuming the role of President. Along this path, I've had the privilege of getting to know extraordinary people, *from both the present and the past!*

I wish to extend my heartfelt thanks to everyone who devoted their time to reading my book, giving feedback, contributing details, providing encouragement, patiently enduring my passionate discussions about the contents, and forgiving my lengthy disappearances due to work on the book.

Lisa Anderson, Gwen Causey, Charles Clemmons, Ellie DeYoung, Diana Fotinatos, Judy Gordon, Bob Hagerman, Tommy Harrelson, Morgan Harper, Col. Willie L. Gore, Randy Jones, Kathryn and Arnold Kalmanson, Pat Kirkman, Debbie Mollycheck, Mary Ellen

Watts Poole, Musette Steck, Bob Surridge, and Ron and Lois (Gore) Thompson.

I'd particularly like to thank Donnie Joyner, who was there every step of the way.

I'd like to give a special thank you to the members of the Clemmons family who shared their family history and who were supportive of me telling this story: Annette Clemmons, Marjorie Clemmons, Michael and Andrea Clemmons, Steven Clemmons, Priscilla Moore, and Joy Smith.

And thank you to Carolyn Evans for bringing Miss Annie to life.

Additionally, I appreciate all of those who attended my history presentations or read my articles and then encouraged me to write a book.

I'd like to thank my family for their support, especially my husband, Bob, for always believing in me.

Finally, I'd like to thank two teachers who made a difference in my life.

My second-grade teacher, Miss Mary Louise Hitchler, typed, mimeographed, and stapled the pages of my first book, "Jack the Dog" and shared it with the entire class. She told me I was a writer.

My eighth-grade American History teacher, Mr. Bob Woodruff, whose explanations of democracy, justice, and the separation of powers, inspired me then, and continue to inspire me to this day. It was the short essay assignments in his class that sparked my desire to write about history.

Thank you and Farewell to Annie Clemmons

ANNIE CLEMMONS DIES

Annie Celmmons, 66, died at her home here Friday, following a long illness. Funeral and burial was held Monday afternoon. Her daughter, the wife of a Naval Lieutenant in California, flew home for the funeral. The decased is also survived by three brothers, George, James and Rufus Clemmons, respected colored resident of Southport.

Figure 11Annie Clemmons obituary, State Port Pilot, Feb. 22, 1956, p. 6

Annie Clemmons passed away on February 17, 1956. Her obituary was written up in the paper but it contains some errors. This is no reflection on the newspaper, as obituaries are notorious for inaccuracies. Annie's son-in-law was in the Army, not the Navy. Her daughter lived in Texas, not California. Her three surviving brothers were George, James, and John (Baby).

But they got the most important thing right:

Annie Clemmons is a respected resident of Southport.

Contact the Author

Every effort has been made to ensure the accuracy of the information in this book. If any reader sees an error, has additional information about Annie Clemmons, or just wants to talk about the history of Southport, I would be interested in hearing from you. I never tire of discussing history!

It was a disappointment in my research that I was never able to find a photo of Annie. If anyone comes across one, please let me know.

I can be reached through the Southport Historical Society www.southporthistoricalsociety.org.

Timeline of this Book

1853 – Allen Clemmons is born into bondage in Lockwood's Folly

1858 – Martha Clemmons is born into bondage in Smithville

1861 – NC secedes from the Union and joins the Confederacy

1865 – Smithville surrenders to Union forces; Lt. Wm. Cushing informs the enslaved people that they are free. (January); Wilmington falls to the Union (February); Lee surrenders at Appomattox (April); 13th Amendment (December)

1867 – 1st meeting of NC Republican Party in Raleigh (March); 1st NC election including Black men as voters (November); Methodist Episcopal Church for the Colored is established in Smithville and trustees buy property in Smithville (December)

1868 – NC ratifies a new constitution and rejoins the Union (April); William Brown becomes first Black man in Smithville to be elected to public office (May); Abraham Galloway elected to state senate (May); KKK comes to North Carolina; 14th Amendment (July)

1870 – 15th Amendment (February); Gov. Holden declares an insurrection due to ongoing Klan violence (April). Abraham Galloway dies. Thousands attend his funeral in Wilmington. (September)

1871 – Gov. William Holden becomes 1st U.S. governor to be impeached, convicted, and removed from office (February)

1873 - 1st NC Klan Amnesty Act

1874 – by this year, Allen Clemmons moves to Smithville, and gets a job on USE dredge boat, *Cape Fear*; Solomon C. Smith is the first Black man to run for mayor of Smithville (June); 1874 – Allen Clemmons and Martha Evans wed (November); NC Klan Amnesty Act expanded to pardon murder, arson and burglary

1876 – NC Constitutional Amendments restricting voting rights

1879 - Allen Clemmons, Jr. is born

1882 – Allen and Martha Clemmons purchase a lot and build a house on E. Brown Street; Charles Henry is born

1885 – Katie is born

1886 – Israel Preston is born

1887 – Smithville changes its name to Southport

1888 – Joseph Anthony is born

1890 – Anna Alene is born

1894 - George Allen is born

1896 - James Franklin is born; Plessy v Ferguson "Separate but equal"

1898 – Wilmington Massacre and Coup (November)

1900 - John Elmore was born; literacy test and poll tax added to NC Constitution (April) Congressman George. H. White submits 1st anti-lynching bill to Congress

1901 – The last Black U.S. Congressman, George H. White, leaves office. Nearly 100% of Black NC men were removed from voting rosters (between 1901 and 1904); NC became part of the "Solid South" consistently voting Democrat.

1911 – Annie becomes a Nurse

1913 – Maggie Louise is born, and Annie becomes a mother

1914 – WWI starts in Europe

1917 – US enters WWI

1918 – "Spanish Flu" pandemic in Southport (October); WWI ends

1919 – NC removes the poll tax as a requirement for voting; Annie's mother, Martha Clemmons dies.

1920 – 19th Amendment (August); Annie Clemmons tries to register (October); Annie initiates correspondence with the National Woman's Party

1921 – Brunswick County Training School#1 burns to the ground (Jan)

1922- Allen Clemmons, Sr. dies

1925 – Brunswick County Training School#2 opens

1930 – Maggie Louise graduates from high school

1941 – U.S. enters WWII

1942? – Maggie Louise marries Walter Dooley

1945 – WWII ends

1948 – 15% of eligible NC Black voters registered

1954 - Brown v. Topeka Bd. Of Education "Separate is not equal"

1955- 14 yr. old Emmett Till was tortured and murdered by white supremacists in Mississippi

1956 – Annie Clemmons passes away

1963 – Southport NAACP founded; Youth Group participates in March on Washington for Jobs and Freedom

1964 - Civil Rights Act passed

1965 – "Bloody Sunday" Protest for Voting Rights in Alabama (March); Voting Rights Act passed; NC and the rest of the South shift support to the conservative Republican Party

1968 – More than 50% of eligible Black NC voters registered

1991- Eva Clayton and Mel Watts become 1st Black U.S. Congressional Representatives from N.C. elected in the 20th Century

1999 – Henry Frye becomes the first Black chief justice on the North Carolina Supreme Court

2008 - Barack Obama elected the first Black President of the United States, only the 2nd Democratic candidate to win N.C. since 1964 when the Civil Rights Act passed. (the other was Jimmy Carter in 1976)

2013 – Shelby County v. Holder reduces the effectiveness of the Voting Rights Act by eliminating the preclearance for voting changes; The next day Senator Tom Apodaca (Rep), Chairman of the North Carolina Senate Rules Committee, publicly stated that the North Carolina Legislature would be moving forward with an omnibus law imposing multiple voting restrictions.

2022- Emmett Till Anti-Lynching Act passes making lynching a federal crime.

Bibliography and Endnotes

Bibliography

The following are some of the books that informed my understanding of the history that affected Annie's life. I recommend them if you want to go deeper into any of the topics touched upon in this book.

Barry, John M. 2004. *The Great Influenza: The Story of the Deadliest Pandemic in History*. 1st ed. New York: Penguin Books.

Bradley, Mark L. 2009. *Bluecoats and Tar Heels: Soldiers and Civilians in Reconstruction North Carolina*. Lexington, KY: University Press of Kentucky.

Carson, Susan S. 1992. *Joshua's Dream: The Story of Old Southport A Town with Two Names*. 1st ed. Southport, North Carolina: Southport Historical Society.

Carson, Susan S., and Jon C. Lewis. eds. 2003. *Joshua's Legacy: Dream Makers of Old Southport*. 1st ed. Southport, North Carolina: Southport Historical Society.

Cecelski, David S. 2012. *The Fire of Freedom: Abraham Galloway and the Slaves' Civil War.* 1st ed. Chapel Hill, North Carolina: The University of North Carolina Press.

Cecelski, David S., and Timothy B. Tyson. 1998. *Democracy Betrayed: The Wilmington Race Riot of 1898 and Its Legacy*. 1st ed. Chapel Hill, North Carolina: The University of North Carolina Press.

DuBois, W.E.B. 2007. *Black Reconstruction in America (The Oxford W. E. B. Du Bois): An Essay Toward a History of the Part Which Black Folk Played in the Attempt to Reconstruct Democracy in America, 1860-1880, Kindle Edition*. 1st ed. New York: Oxford University Press.

Evans, William M. 1995. *Ballots and Fence Rails: Reconstruction on the Lower Cape Fear*. Athens, GA: University of Georgia Press.

Foner, Eric. 1988. *Reconstruction: America's Unfinished Revolution (1863-1877)*. 1st ed. New York: HarperCollins Publishers.

Foner, Eric. 2019. *The Second Founding: How the Civil War and Reconstruction Remade the Constitution*. 1st ed. New York: W. W. Norton and Co.

Gilmore, Glenda E. 2019. *Gender and Jim Crow, Second Edition: Women and the Politics of White Supremacy in North Carolina, 1896-1920*. Chapel Hill, NC: University of North Carolina Press.

Jones, Martha S. 2020. *Vanguard: How Black Women Broke Barriers, Won the Vote, and Insisted on Equality for All*. 1st ed. New York: Hachette Book Group.

Justesen, Benjamin R. 2001. *George Henry White: An Even Chance in the Race of Life*. 7th ed. Baton Rouge, LA: Louisiana State University Press.

Kousser, J. Morgan. 1974. *The Shaping of Southern Politics: Suffrage Restriction and the Establishment of the One-party South, 1880-1910*. United Kingdom: Yale University Press.

Krugler, David F. 2014. *1919, The Year of Racial Violence: How African Americans Fought Back, Kindle Edition*. 1st ed. New York: Cambridge University Press.

Leloudis, James L., and Robert R. Korstad. 2020. *Fragile Democracy: The Struggle over Race and Voting Rights in North Carolina*. 1st ed. Chapel Hill, North Carolina: University of North Carolina Press.

Paschal, Richard. 2020. *Jim Crow in North Carolina: The Legislative Program from 1865 to 1920*. 1st ed. Durham, North Carolina: Carolina Academic Press.

Trelease, Allen W. 2023. *White Terror: The Ku Klux Klan Conspiracy and Southern Reconstruction Paperback Reissue*. Baton Rouge, LA: LSU Press.

Umfleet, LaRae. 2020. *A Day of Blood: The 1898 Wilmington Race Riot*. Wilmington, North Carolina: North Carolina Office of Archives and History.

Whitaker, Robert. 2009. *On the Laps of Gods: The Red Summer of 1919 and the Struggle for Justice That Remade a Nation*. 1st ed. New York: Random House.

Ware, Susan. 2020. *Why They Marched: Untold Stories of the Women Who Fought for the Right to Vote*. Cambridge, MA: Belknap Press: An Imprint of Harvard University Press.

Endnotes

[1] The assertion that a Methodist Episcopal minister was also a slaveholder was not done lightly. The Methodist Church took a strong stand against slavery. As early as 1780 the church was preaching against slavery. Thereafter, the North Carolina Methodists adopted antislavery statements insisting Methodists free any slaves they owned. Many Northern abolitionists were Methodist. But then in 1844, foreshadowing the split of the Union, the Methodist Church split over the issue of slavery. Southern churches formed the Methodist Episcopal Church, South. When researching the background of Annie's grandmother, Mary Moore, I searched for all Moores on the slave schedule in Brunswick County. Wm. M.D. Moore is the only Moore listed on the slave schedule in Smithville in 1860. He enslaved 5 adults and 7 children in two slave houses including a 2-year-old female who likely was Annie's mother, Martha Evans (Martha's last name came from her father). Moore's occupation in 1860 is listed as M.E. Minister. Wm. M.D. Moore is on the 1850 slave schedule and census as well. At that time, he was living in Town Creek and listed his occupation as Meth. Minister. He enslaved 5 adults and 3 children. The only other Moore on the slave schedule in Brunswick County in 1860 was James Moore in Northwest who enslaved 50 individuals including a 2-year-old girl. That little girl could be Martha, but it's less likely due to the distance from Smithville. Per local church history, Wm. M.D. Moore was minister of Trinity Methodist church from 1865-1867 which was after the Civil War, at which time he would no longer have been a slaveholder. It's possible before then he was a minister at a different church or was a circuit minister. Moore also served as clerk of the court and owned property near Bonnet's Creek. Seventh Census of the United States (1850): Brunswick County, N.C.; 1850 U.S. Federal Census - Slave Schedules; Eighth Census of the United States (1860): Brunswick County, N.C.;1850 U.S. Federal Census - Slave Schedules. Reaves, Bill. 1978. *Southport (Smithville) A Chronology Volume 1 (1520 - 1887)*. 2nd ed. Wilmington North Carolina: Broadfoot Publishing.; North Carolina, U.S., Marriage Records, 1741-2011 Record.; North Carolina Land Grants. Microfilm publication, 770 rolls. North Carolina State Archives, Raleigh, North Carolina.

[2] Edward Clemmons is the only Clemmons on the 1860 Brunswick County slave schedule that lists a 6- or 7-year-old male. Clemmons enslaved 5 adults and 16 children in two slave houses including a 6-year-old male who is likely Allen. Eighth Census of the United States (1860): Brunswick County, N.C., Slave Schedules, NA.

[3] The National Archives in Washington, DC; Washington, DC, USA; Records of the Assistant Commissioner For the State of North Carolina, Bureau of Refugees, Freedmen, and Abandoned Lands, 1865-1870; NARA Series Number: M843; NARA Reel Number: 27; NARA Record G

[4] "Uncle Frank Gordon Taught School for Fifty-five Years." *The State Port Pilot* (Southport, North Carolina), October 30, 1935.

[5] Ibid.

[6] In 1818 The Slaves and Free Persons of Color Act was amended to state that no slave shall teach another slave to read or write. In 1831 following Nat Turner's rebellion, the sanction was expanded to restrict anyone from teaching slaves to read or write. The rationale stated in the act was that "the teaching of slaves to read and write has a tendency to excite dissatisfaction in their minds and to produce insurrection and rebellion to the manifest injury of the citizens of this state."

[7] Steck, Musette. Phone conversation with the author, January 7, 2024.

[8] U.S., Freedmen's Bureau Records, 1865-1878 ("Solomon C. Smith")

[9] U.S., Freedmen's Bureau Records, 1865-1878 (December 1867, William Brown); This purchase makes it appear that the Church congregation was prospering. However, a letter from their minister written at the same time indicates that the congregants were suffering financial hardships. *"We are not doing so well here the people of Smithville are very poor so much so that they cannot support me as their preacher for the last three months I have not had but $8.78 cents from my congregation I do not know how I shall get along at this rate for the times is hard here"*, Letter from Rev. Abram G. Smith to an unknown party. September 25, 1867". U.S., Freedmen's Bureau Records, 1865-1878 (A.G. Smith).

[10] Reaves, Bill. 1978. *A Chronology of Smithville/Southport, Volume 1*. 2nd ed. Wilmington, North Carolina: Broadfoot Publishing Company, p. 49, 58.

[11] This is an assumption due to both families being members of the Methodist Episcopal church. In the previously referenced 1867 deed filed with the Freedmen's Bureau, the trustees mentioned forming a school at the church. Separately, the 1867 Freemen's Bureau records listed Sol. And Abram Smith as teachers. Frank Gordon maintained a friendship with Sol. Smith all his life even after leaving Smithville. Smith married Gordon and his wife. Then in 1904, long after moving away from Smithville, Smith sold his home in Smithville to Gordon's oldest son, Cenelius, for "the love and affection he had for him plus $1" indicating an ongoing warm relationship between the families. North Carolina, Marriage Records, 1741-2011(April 8, 1879)Brunswick County Register of Deeds: Real Property Book: VV 260.

[12] Ninth Census of the United States (1870): Smithville, N.C.

[13] North Carolina, U.S., Marriage Records, 1741-2011 (November 28, 1874).

[14] U.S., Register of Civil, Military, and Naval Service, 1863-1959(1818).

[15] "The Way It Was." *The State Port Pilot* (New York), October 2, 1968.

[16] U.S., Register of Civil, Military, and Naval Service, 1863-1959 (1903).

[17] "The Way It Was." *The State Port Pilot* (New York), October 30, 1991.

[18] U.S., Register of Civil, Military, and Naval Service, 1863-1959 (1881)

[19]"The Way It Was." *The State Port Pilot* (New York), October 2, 1968.

[20] Tenth Census of the United States (1880): Brunswick County, N.C

[21]Brunswick County Register of Deeds: Real Property Book: AA 176

[22]Record of Wills, Ca. 1790-1946; Cross Index to Wills, 1764-1946; Author: North Carolina. Superior Court (Brunswick County); Probate Place: Brunswick, North Carolina

[23]Brunswick County Register of Deeds: Real Property Book: AA 133

[24] The property was sold in 2023.

[25] Brown owned a 50-acre farm outside of Smithville not too far from Price Creek Range Light. He, his wife, and their eight children ran the farm. The family composed ten of the sixteen free Blacks living in Smithville Township in 1860. At that time about one-tenth of the Black population in North Carolina was free, equaling about 30,453. "Official Headquarters Second Military District." *The Daily Standard* (Raleigh, NC), May 21, 1868. "Brunswick County-Official." *The Weekly Star* (Wilmington, NC), August 12, 1870.

[26] Ninth Census of the United States (1870): Smithville, N.C

[27] Brunswick County Register of Deeds: Real Property Book: Y 577; National Registration of Historic Places, John N. Smith Cemetery, BW0337, listed 8/9/2021.

[28] "Frauds and Falsehoods." *The Daily Journal* (Wilmington, NC), May 5, 1868.

[29] Ninth Census of the United States (1870): Smithville, N.C

[30] "Southport Locals." *The Southport Leader* (Southport, NC), March 23, 1893.

[31] "Southport Locals." *The Southport Leader* (Southport, NC), June 29, 1893.

[32] Letter to Dr. J. T. Denning, Brunswick County Superintendent of Public Schools from the Executive Committee of the Southport Colored Citizens League (Herbert Brown, Elmer Davis, (Mrs.) Dollie Evans, Ephraim Swain), Oct. 22, 1949. Archives of the Susan Carson Research Room, Southport Historical Society.

[33] Allen Clemmons' gravestone in John N. Smith Cemetery contains the Masonic symbol indicating that he was a member.

[34] Brunswick County School Board Agenda and Minutes Archives (bcswan.net)

[35] Ninth Census of the United States (1870): Smithville, N.C; North Carolina, Marriage Records, 1741-2011

[36] U.S., Appointments of U. S. Postmasters, 1832-1971

[37] "The Colored Republicans." *The Southport Leader* (Southport, NC), January 14, 1892.

[38] "Attention Republicans." *The Southport Leader* (Southport, NC), October 22, 1896.

[39]Tenth Census of the United States (1880): Brunswick County, N.C

[40] "Republican Primaries in Brunswick." *The Wilmington Morning Star* (New York), September 26, 1886. The other representatives were John Evans, a trustee of St. James AMEZ church, Robert C. Smith, a local Black carpenter. A town

committee was also set up that included William Brown, Jr. and Robert C. Smith. The head of the committee was S.P. Swain, a local White Republican.

[41]"Uncle Frank Gordon Died at His Home Here Sunday." *The State Port Pilot* (New York), April 19, 1939.

[42] Price, Michael L. 2011. *Journey to Cape Fear: The Prices of Brunswick County Their Related Families and Their Journey from Old Europe to Cape Fear.* Scotts Valley, CA: CreateSpace. P. 228-229.

[43]Reaves, Bill. 1978. *A Chronology of Smithville/Southport, Volume 1.* 2nd ed. Wilmington, North Carolina: Broadfoot Publishing Company, p. 62.

[44] "Brunswick Republicans." *The Wilmington Morning Star* (Wilmington, North Carolina), June 23, 1874.

[45] "Editor Wilmington Post." *The Wilmington Post* (Wilmington, NC), September 15, 1876.

[46] Reaves, Bill. 1998. *A Chronology of Smithville/Southport, Volume 2 (1887-1920).* 2nd printing. Southport, North Carolina: Southport Historical Society, p. 2.

[47] For a fuller analysis of the Election of 1898 and the strategy of White Supremacy to advance the Democratic Party, see Cecelski, David S., and Timothy B. Tyson. 1998. *Democracy Betrayed: The Wilmington Race Riot of 1898 and Its Legacy.* Chapel Hill: University of North Carolina Press.

[48] Hayden, Harry. 1936. *The Story of the Wilmington Rebellion.* Wilmington, North Carolina: H. Hayden. Pp. 6-8

[49] Connor, R. D. W. 1913. *A Manual of North Carolina for the Use of the Members of the General Assembly.* Wilmington, North Carolina: North Carolina Historical Commission. p. 1010

[50] Twelfth Census of the United States (1880): Brunswick County, N.C

[51] Skilled enslaved people, especially in coastal North Carolina, were sometimes permitted to hire themselves out for wages. For example. Abraham Galloway was a master brick mason and his enslaver, Milton Hankins, permitted him to hire himself out for brick-laying jobs as long as he turned over fifteen dollars a month. One of the benefits of freedom for Allen Galloway and other freedmen who didn't work as sharecroppers was the ability to keep all their own earnings. Cecelski, David S. 2012. *The Fire of Freedom: Abraham Galloway and the Slaves' Civil War.* 1st ed. Chapel Hill, North Carolina: The University of North Carolina Press.

[52] Statistics calculated by the author from the Twelfth Census of the United States (1900): Smithville Township, N.C.

[53] Ibid.

[54] The 1900 statewide literacy rate for Black North Carolinians age 10 and over was 52.4%. Southport's 1900 literacy rate for adults 18 and over was 56%. If school-age children 10 – 17 were included, this would be even higher. *Second Annual Catalogue of the North Carolina State Colored Normal Schools for 1905-06. 1906.* Raleigh, N.C. Southport Statistics calculated by the author from the Twelfth Census of the United States (1900): Smithville Township, N.C. *"Uncle Frank Gordon Taught School for Fifty-five Years."* The State Port Pilot (Southport, NC), October 30, 1935.

[55] Sarah is the only person in her age cohort with a 4-year high school education. Analysis conducted by the author from the Sixteenth Census of the United States (1940): Smithville Township, N.C.

[56] Southport historical tradition. Tuition at the Normal school was free for students who would go on to teach Black students. It's believed that Sarah's mother and brother helped pay for her travel and other expenses.

[57] "First Retirement in the County." *State Port Pilot* (Southport, NC), November 25, 1942.

[58] Statistics calculated by the author from the Twelfth Census of the United States (1900): Smithville Township, N.C

[59] For a fuller discussion see Umfleet, LaRae. 2020. *A Day of Blood: The 1898 Wilmington Race Riot.* Wilmington, North Carolina: North Carolina Office of Archives and History.

[60] Clawson, Thomas W., active 1898. Thomas W. Clawson Papers, 1898 manuscript.p.9

[61] U.S., World War I Draft Registration Cards, 1917-1918

[62] Newspapers at the time referred to the pandemic of 1918 as an epidemic of influenza or Spanish Flu so that's how it is referred to in Annie's speech or thoughts. However, those terms are not accurate. The influenza outbreak of 1918 – 1919 was a global pandemic exacerbated by the World War. It was often called the Spanish Flu because Spain was one of the few countries not involved in the war and so their newspapers made regular reports on the prevalence of the disease. Countries such as the U.S., France, and Germany tended to suppress the extent of illness so as not to appear vulnerable to their enemies. Because Spain was reporting its statistics accurately, the common belief at the time was that the illness originated in Spain, hence the name "Spanish Flu".

[63] Reaves, Bill. 1998. *Southport (Smithville) A Chronology Volume 2 (1887 - 1920).* Southport Historical Society.

[64] "Dr. Watson's Advice." *The Wilmington Morning Star* (Wilmington, NC), September 29, 1918. p.7.

[65] "Fort Caswell Lifts Quarantine." *The Wilmington Morning Star* (Wilmington, NC), November 3, 1918.

[66] "Southport Escaped Lightly." *The Wilmington Morning Star* (Wilmington, NC), November 4, 1918.

[67] "Influenza Over at Fort and in City." *The Wilmington Morning Star* (Wilmington, NC), October 19, 1918.

[68] "Influenza Took Heavy Toll During October." *News and Record* (Greensboro, NC), October 20, 1918. Peek, Matthew M. "List of North Carolina's Dead WWI Service Individuals." Https://www.Dncr.Nc.Gov/Blog/. November 15, 2018.

[69] This certificate was mentioned by Annie in her second letter to Miss Wold.

[70] Sixteenth Census of the United States (1920): Brunswick County, N.C.

[71] Joyner, Donnie. Conversations with Clemmons family members Steven Clemmons, Pricilla Moore, Joy Smith, and Michael Clemmons, July 21-22, 2022.

[72] This lot was in a parcel of nine blocks of land owned by Dr. O.F. Swasey originally from New England. Dr. Swasey's property was divided into 100 small building lots. The majority of these were eventually purchased by Southport's Black citizens, forming a tight-knit community of homes and small businesses.

[73] Joyner, Donnie. Conversations with Clemmons family members Steven Clemmons, Pricilla Moore, Joy Smith, and Michael Clemmons, July 21-22, 2022.

[74] Due to the destruction of many of Brunswick County Training School's records, Maggie Louise's graduation date had to be estimated. It's based on her age and the date that BCT was established.

[75] In one of many instances in which the small town of Smithville/Southport brushes up against history, it's possible that Annie's parents, Allen and Martha Clemmons may at some point have passed a young Woodrow Wilson on the street. Wilson moved to Wilmington with his parents in 1874, the same year Allen and Martha got married. Seventeen-year-old Tommy (as he was then known) was fascinated with the Cape Fear River. Southport oral tradition is that he would sometimes come downriver to Smithville and stay at the Stuart Inn. No one would have guessed that the awkward teen would someday have such a profound impact on their lives.

[76] "Woman Suffrage and the Negro." *The Wilmington Morning Star* (Wilmington, North Carolina), June 28, 1920.

[77] "Woman Suffrage Ensures South's White Supremacy." *The Wilmington Morning Star* (Wilmington, NC), January 7, 1918.

[78] "Suffragists Will Invade Southport." *The Wilmington Morning Star*, June 6, 1920. "Suffrage Folks To Meet Here June 15." *Fayetteville Observer* (Fayetteville, NC), June 10, 1920. "Woman Developing Plan of Campaign." *The New Bern Sun Journal* (New Bern, North Carolina), June 11, 1920.

[79] *The Wilmington Morning Star* (Wilmington, NC), October 13, 1920.

[80] Ibid. The Army Navy Club, created during WWI was in the first floor of the Masonic Lodge on Nash St.

[81] Ibid.; *The Wilmington Morning Star* (Wilmington, NC), October 27, 1920.

[82] *The Wilmington Morning Star* (Wilmington, NC), October 19, 1920.

[83] "Votes of Women Near Forty Percent of Total." *The Wilmington Morning Star* (Wilmington, North Carolina), October 24, 1920.

[84] National Woman's Party Papers, 1913-1974, Library of Congress (Microfilm (1979), reel 5). Note: Anna signs her letter "Clemons". There is some evidence that some members of her family spelled their last name with a single "m" during that time period. John Elmore Clemmons, Annie's youngest brother, signed his draft card Clemons. All of the other brothers signed Clemmons. Both Annie's parents, Allen and Martha, have Clemons on their grave markers. It appears that over time the family transitioned to the spelling of "Clemmons", which is how it is spelled on Annie's grave marker. Thus, the more standard spelling of Clemmons has been used in this book except in the signature line of Annie's letters.

[85] Whitaker, Robert. 2008. *On The Laps of Gods: The Red Summer of 1919 and the Struggle for Justice that Remade a Nation*. New York: Crown Publishers.

[86] "Year's Lynchings Claim 82 Victims." *The Wilmington Morning Star* (Wilmington, North Carolina), January 1, 1920.

[87] Rosenwald-Fisk.edu

[88] Founded in 1917 by Julius Rosenwald and his family, the Rosenwald Fund, also known as the Julius Rosenwald Foundation, was a philanthropic institution. During the 1910s to the 1930s, its principal focus centered on education in North Carolina. Through matching grants, the fund facilitated the construction of over 800 public school buildings intended specifically for African American children in NC.

[89] Joyner, Donnie. Conversations with Clemmons family members Steven Clemmons, Pricilla Moore, Joy Smith, and Michael Clemmons, July 21-22, 2022.

[90] Ibid.

[91] Judgement Annie A Clemmons v. Malissie Jackson, et al. Brunswick County, NC, Superior Court, June 24, 1922. Brunswick Property B36 p272-273

[92] Joyner, Donnie. Conversations with Clemmons family members Steven Clemmons, Pricilla Moore, Joy Smith, and Michael Clemmons, July 21-22, 2022.

[93] For Brunswick County Training School#1, it was necessary to raise a total of $8,920 ($142,000 in 2023) Contributions were made by Blacks: $2,000.00, Whites: $1,300.00, Public funds: $4,420.00 and Rosenwald fund: $1200.00. For Brunswick County Training School#2, it was necessary to raise a total of $11,274 ($200,000 in 2023). Contributions were made by Blacks: $5,050.00, Whites: $1,499.00, Public funds: $3,325.00 and Rosenwald fund: $1,500. Rosenwald $1,200.00. Rosenwald-Fisk.edu

[94] "Six Go To Oglethorpe; Have Lunch Together Before Boarding Train." *The Knoxville News* (Knoxville, TN), December 14, 1940.

[95] "Dooley." *El Paso Times* (El Paso, TX), July 16, 1992.

[96] "Dooley." *El Paso Times* (El Paso, TX), December 13, 2007.

[97] Joyner, Donnie. Conversations with Clemmons family members Steven Clemmons, Pricilla Moore, Joy Smith, and Michael Clemmons, July 21-22, 2022.

[98] Seventeenth Census of the United States (1920): Brunswick County, N.C.

[99] Carson, Susan S., and Jon C. Lewis. eds. 2003. *Joshua's Legacy: Dream Makers of Old Southport*. 1st ed. Southport, North Carolina: Southport Historical Society.

[100] "History of the Southport-Brunswick County Chapter Of the National Association for the Advancement of Colored People 'The Untold Story'", 1989. Susan Carson Research Room, Southport Historical Society

[101] U.S., Register of Civil, Military, and Naval Service, 1863-1959; North Carolina, Marriage Records, 1741-2011

[102] Eighteenth Census of the United States (1930): Brunswick County, N.C.

[103] U.S., Register of Civil, Military, and Naval Service, 1863-1959; North Carolina, Marriage Records, 1741-2011; Eighteenth Census of the United States (1930): Brunswick County, N.C.

[104] Eighteenth Census of the United States (1930): Brunswick County, N.C

[105] Nineteenth Census of the United States (1940): Brunswick County, N.C., U.S., School Yearbooks, 1900-2016: Livingstone College Yearbook (1983), p. 158. "Sheriff James Clemmons, Jr. Obituary." www.Mcmillanfh.Com. August 6, 2021.

[106] North Carolina, World War I Service Cards, 1917-1919; Eighteenth Census of the United States (1930): Brunswick County, N.C. Memories of "Miss Julia" and her store are from an email between Judy Gordon and the author, Jan 4, 2024.

[107] Nineteenth Census of the United States (1930): Brunswick County, N.C.

[108] Public Laws of North Carolina, session of 1866, p. 99; and Senate Ex. Doc. no. 26, 39 Cong., 1 Sess., p. 197. March 10, 1866.

[109] U.S. Const. (Article I, Section 5)

[110] For a full discussion of the life of Abraham Galloway see Cecelski, David S. 2012. *The Fire of Freedom: Abraham Galloway and the Slaves' Civil War.* 1st ed. Chapel Hill, North Carolina: The University of North Carolina Press.

[111] Connor, R. D. W. 1913. *A Manual of North Carolina for the Use of the Members of the General Assembly*. Wilmington, North Carolina: North Carolina Historical Commission. p. 1010

[112] Kalb, Deborah. 2016. *Guide to U.S. Elections*. 7th ed. Thousand Oaks, CA: CQ Press, p.1718.

[113] "Proceedings of the Convention." *The Daily Standard* (Southport, North Carolina), January 17, 1868. P.2

[114] For a fuller discussion of Abraham Galloway, see Cecelski, David S. 2012. *The Fire of Freedom: Abraham Galloway and the Slaves' Civil War*. Chapel Hill, North Carolina: University of North Carolina Press.

[115] U.S., Freedmen's Bureau Records, 1865-1878 (Rev. A G Smith. 27 July 1867)

[116] Letter from Judge Albion W. Tourgee to Senator Joseph Abbott dated May 24, 1870.

[117] DeRosset, William L. 1938. *Pictorial and Historical New Hanover County and Wilmington North Carolina 1723 - 1938*. Wilmington, North Carolina: Published by the Author.

[118] "Ku Klux - The Avenger Abroad" Newspapers.com. The Daily Journal, Wilmington, NC. April 18, 1868. p. 3.

[119] "Genuine Insolence" Newspapers.com. The Daily Journal, Wilmington, NC. April 21, 1868. p.3; Evans, William McKee, Ballots & Fence Rails: Reconstruction on the Lower Cape Fear. Chapel Hill, University of North Carolina Press, 1967.

[120] "Editor Wilmington Post." Wilmington Post (Wilmington, North Carolina), September 15, 1876.

[121] Letter from Judge Sam W. Watts to Governor William W. Holden on August 14, 1869. State Archives of North Carolina. Watts was frustrated after a trial in which two white men had stolen a horse from a well-respected Black man. "in all my life I never saw a jury so disregard their oaths and bring in such a villainous decision". In this particular case, he was sure that the men were probably wanted for other crimes, so he held them for several days and requested that Holden let him know if they were on his list of wanted men. Watts, who moved to Southport with his family toward the end of his career, was widely known for trying to hold fair trials despite being continuously thwarted by Klan-sympathizing juries. For this, he was slandered in the Democratic press especially by Josiah Turner who was a strong supporter of the Klan. Turner was widely known for mocking Republicans and those who worked against the Klan, often giving them derisive nicknames. In Watts' case, he continually referred to him in the press as "Greasy Sam".

[122] Forty years after Outlaw's death, a monument was erected in the Graham Courthouse square near the place of his lynching. The monument which glorifies the Confederate States of America consists of a 30-foot-high column topped by a Confederate soldier standing at parade rest looking north. Repeated attempts by the NAACP to have the statue removed have been dismissed.

[123] Massengill, Stephen E. "The Detectives of William W. Holden, 1869-1870." *The North Carolina Historical Review* 62, no. 4 (1985): 448–87. http://www.jstor.org/stable/23518497.

[124] "The Legislature of North Carolina." *The Wilmington Post* (Wilmington, North Carolina), December 19, 1869.

[125] Text of "Shoffner Act" as quoted in Trial of William W. Holden, Governor of North Carolina, before the Senate of North Carolina. United States: "Sentinel" printing office, 1871.

[126] Brisson, Jim D. "'Civil Government Was Crumbling Around Me': The Kirk-Holden War of 1870." *The North Carolina Historical Review* 88, no. 2 (2011): 123–63. http://www.jstor.org/stable/23523540.

[127] "Respected Middle Township Farmer Goes to His Long Home." *The Republican* (Danville, Indiana), April 28, 1910.

[128] An Act for Amnesty and Pardon, Ch. 181, Public Laws and Resolutions Together with the Private Laws of the State of North Carolina Passed by the General Assembly at its Session, 1872 – 73. An Act to Amend An Act for Amnesty and Pardon, Ch.20, Laws and resolutions of the State of North Carolina, passed by the General Assembly at its session [1874-1875]

[129] *The Daily Journal* (Wilmington, NC), September 3, 1870 p.3; *The Daily Journal* (Wilmington, NC), September 3, 1870 p.3.

[130] The Statistics of the Population of the United States in 1870 Embracing the Tables of Race, Nationality, Sex, Selected Ages and Occupations...compiled from the Original Returns of the Ninth Census under the Secretary of the Interior. 1872. Washington DC: Government Printing Office, p.221.

[131] "19th Century Black Congress Member Biographies." Avoice. Congressional Black Caucus Foundation, Accessed August 10, 2023. https://avoice.cbcfinc.org/.

[132] Justesen, Benjamin R. 2001. *George Henry White: An Even Chance in the Race of Life.* 7th ed. Baton Rouge, LA: Louisiana State University Press.

[133] Constitution of the State of North Carolina as amended by the Constitutional Convention of 1875, Section VI.

[134] Constitution of the State of North Carolina as amended by the Constitutional Convention of 1875, Section VI.

[135] "The Entire Democratic Ticket Goes in Again." *The Southport Leader* (Southport, North Carolina), November 10, 1892. P. 4

[136] Ibid.

[137] "The General Assembly." *The News and Observer* (Raleigh, NC), February 16, 1893.

[138] Public Laws and Resolutions of the State of North Carolina, Passed by the General Assembly of the Session of 1895. Law 211, Ch. 159. NCLeg.gov.

[139] Kousser, J. Morgan. *The Shaping of Southern Politics: Suffrage Restriction and the Establishment of the One-party South, 1880-1910.* United Kingdom: Yale University Press, 1974. Supra note 72 at 187.

[140] Ibid. p. 42.

[141] "They Don't Relish the Appointment of Pop. Maynard." *The Messenger and Intelligencer* (Wadesboro, NC), May 23, 1895.

[142] "A Deceptive Letter Writer." *The Wilmington Messenger* (Wilmington, North Carolina), October 12, 1898, p. 4. note: The names of the three aldermen were Elijah Green, John Norwood, and Andrew Walker (later a Major in Spanish American War).

[143] For a full discussion of the events in Wilmington in 1898 see Umfleet, LaRae. 2020. *A Day of Blood: The 1898 Wilmington Race Riot*. Wilmington, North Carolina: North Carolina Office of Archives and History and Umfleet, LaRae. 2006. *1898 Wilmington Race Riot Report*. Raleigh, NC: North Carolina Dept. of Cultural Resources, Wilmington Race Riot Commission.

[144] Daniels, Josephus. 1941. *Editor in Politics*. Kindle ed. Chapel Hill: The University of North Carolina Press.

[145] "Sizzling Talk: Most Remarkable Speech by the Hon. A. M. Waddell." *The Semi-Weekly Messenger* (Wilmington, North Carolina), October 28, 1898.

[146] Umfleet, LaRae. 2006. *1898 Wilmington Race Riot Report*. Wilmington, North Carolina: NC Dept. of Cultural Resources.

[147] Hayden, Harry. 1936. *The Story of the Wilmington Rebellion*. Wilmington, North Carolina: H. Hayden.

[148] "Citizens Aroused: Large Mass Meeting of Business Men Held in the Court House." *The Wilmington Morning Star* (Wilmington, North Carolina), November 10, 1898.

[149] Umfleet, LaRae. 2006. *1898 Wilmington Race Riot Report*. Wilmington, North Carolina: NC Dept. of Cultural Resources.

[150] Hayden, Harry. 1936. *The Story of the Wilmington Rebellion*. Wilmington, North Carolina: H. Hayden.

[151] Justesen, Benjamin R. 2001. *George Henry White: An Even Chance in the Race of Life*. 1st ed. Baton Rouge, LA: Louisiana State University Press.

[152] Anonymous to William McKinley, 13 November 1898, file 17743-1898, Department of Justice, Record Group R660, National Archives, Washington, D.C.

[153] "The Story of the Wilmington, N.C. Race Riots." *Collier's* (New York), November 26, 1898.

[154] Between 1900 and 2022 over 200 anti-lynching bills were submitted to Congress. It wasn't until 2022 that the Emmit Till anti-lynching bill passed. (The bill was named after a 14-year-old boy who was brutally murdered by a ruthless mob in 1955).

[155] Connor, R. D. W. 1913. *A Manual of North Carolina for the Use of the Members of the General Assembly*. Wilmington, North Carolina: North Carolina Historical Commission. p. 1016

[156] On August 2, 1900, the North Carolina gubernatorial election took place, resulting in Charles Brantley Aycock, the Democratic nominee, securing victory over Spencer B. Adams, the Republican nominee, with 59.57% of the total votes. Aycock's win marked the beginning of a series of 18 successive elections where the Democratic candidate consistently claimed the Governor's seat. In Brunswick County, Aycock lost to the Republican candidate, 915 – 948. Aycock won in New Hanover, 2963 – 3, the low Republican vote a residual impact from the 1898

Massacre. "The Vote On The Amendment And For Governor." *Wilmington Morning Star* (Wilmington, North Carolina), August 28, 1900.

[157] Ibid.p.1017

[158] "A Renewed Effort to Repeal the Literacy Test in North Carolina." Spectrum News One. March 13, 2023. www.spectrumlocalnews.com

[159] Calvo , Mariana , and Jennifer Colton. "Henry Frye - Change from the Inside." The Meaning of a Vote. Duke University, April 17, 2016. https://sites.duke.edu/pjms364s_01_s2016/.

[160]. "Judicial Heros and Legends: March 10, 2021 Chief Justice Henry E. Frye." The National Judicial College. March 10, 2021. www.judges.org.

[161] "Current Conditions of Voting Rights Discrimination in North Carolina Prepared by Forward Justice." Report at House Committee on the Judiciary: Potential Legislative Reforms, Leadership Conference on Civil and Human Rights, August 6, 2021.

[162] History and Enforcement of the Voting Rights Act of 1965: Hearing before the Subcommittee on the Constitution, Civil Rights, and Civil Liberties, 116th Cong. (2019) https://www.govinfo.gov/content/pkg/CHRG-116hhrg39677/html/CHRG-116hhrg39677.htm

Made in the USA
Middletown, DE
02 February 2024

48449532R00096